MANAGING
ECONOMIC CRISIS
IN EAST ASIA

The **Saw Centre for Financial Studies** was established at the National University of Singapore on 1 December 2003. The Centre is named after a distinguished NUS alumnus Professor Saw Swee-Hock, whose generous endowed gift has enabled the founding of this Centre. The Saw Centre is situated within the vibrant community of the renowned NUS Business School.

The Saw Centre's purpose is to conduct quality research, educational activities and training programmes related to the financial services industry in the Asia Pacific region. With the resources of the university and active contribution from industry professionals, it is a resource centre that will benefit both academics and practitioners.

The **East Asian Institute (EAI)** was set up in April 1997 as an autonomous research organization under a statute of the National University of Singapore. It is the successor of the former Institute of East Asian Political Economy (IEAPE), which was itself the successor of the Institute of East Asian Philosophies (IEAP), originally established by Dr Goh Keng Swee in 1983 for the study of Confucianism. The main mission of EAI is to promote academic and policy-oriented research on contemporary China, including Hong Kong, Taiwan and Macau, and other East Asian economies. The long-term vision of EAI is to develop into the region's foremost research institution on East Asian development, with a strong focus on China. For more information on EAI, please visit <www.eai.nus.edu.sg>.

The **Institute of Southeast Asian Studies (ISEAS)** was established as an autonomous organization in 1968. It is a regional centre dedicated to the study of socio-political, security and economic trends and developments in Southeast Asia and its wider geostrategic and economic environment. The Institute's research programmes are the Regional Economic Studies (RES, including ASEAN and APEC), Regional Strategic and Political Studies (RSPS), and Regional Social and Cultural Studies (RSCS).

ISEAS Publishing, an established academic press, has issued more than 2,000 books and journals. It is the largest scholarly publisher of research about Southeast Asia from within the region. ISEAS Publishing works with many other academic and trade publishers and distributors to disseminate important research and analyses from and about Southeast Asia to the rest of the world.

MANAGING
ECONOMIC CRISIS
IN EAST ASIA

EDITED BY
SAW SWEE-HOCK AND **JOHN WONG**

EAI

First published in Singapore in 2010 by ISEAS Publishing
Institute of Southeast Asian Studies
30 Heng Mui Keng Terrace
Pasir Panjang
Singapore 119614
E-mail: publish@iseas.edu.sg
Website: http://bookshop.iseas.edu.sg

jointly with
Saw Centre for Financial Studies
NUS Business School
National University of Singapore
BIZ 2 Building, #04-01
1 Business Link
Singapore 117592

and
East Asian Institute
National University of Singapore
469A Bukit Timah Road
Tower Block #06-01
Singapore 259770

The responsibility for facts and opinions in this publication rests exclusively with the authors and their interpretations do not necessarily reflect the views or the policy of the publishers or their supporters.

ISEAS Library Cataloguing-in-Publication Data

Managing economic crisis in East Asia / edited by Saw Swee-Hock and John Wong.
  1. Global Financial Crisis, 2008–2009.
  2. Financial crises—East Asia.
  3. Financial crises—China.
  4. Foreign exchange—Government policy—East Asia.
  5. Foreign exchange—Government policy—China.
  I. Saw, Swee-Hock, 1931–
  II. Wong, John, 1939–
HB3816.5 M26   2010

ISBN 978-981-230-972-3 (soft cover)
ISBN 978-981-4311-18-2 (hard cover)
ISBN 978-981-4279-01-7 (E-book PDF)

Typeset by Superskill Graphics Pte Ltd
Printed in Singapore by Utopia Press Pte Ltd

Contents

List of Tables

List of Figures

Preface

In November 2009, the Saw Centre for Financial Studies, NUS Business School, and the East Asian Institute, National University of Singapore, jointly organized the International Conference on Managing Economic Crisis in East Asia. The seven chapters included in this book consist of a selection of the papers presented in the conference, and subsequently revised for publication. Chapter 1 was specifically written by the volume editors to present the salient features of the important subject covered in the book.

We would like to thank the chapter writers for their excellent cooperation for presenting their papers in the conference and, more importantly, for revising the papers for publication. Our appreciation also goes to Mrs Triena Ong of ISEAS Publications Unit for overseeing the expeditious publication of the book. We are delighted for ISEAS to be a co-publisher.

Saw Swee-Hock and John Wong

The Contributors

Francis T. Lui is Professor of Economics at the Hong Kong University of Science and Technology. He is also Director of the Centre for Economic Development at the University. His research interests include economic growth, social security, exchange rate system, the Hong Kong economy and the Chinese economy. He served as a member of the Long Term Housing Strategy Advisory Committee, Mandatory Provident Fund Schemes Appeal Board, and the Task Force Employment of the Hong Kong SAR Government. His major publications are *Old-Age Retirement Protection: A Plan for Hong Kong* and *Industrial Development in Singapore, Taiwan and South Korea*. He obtained his Ph.D. from the University of Minnesota.

Qian Meijun is an Assistant Professor at the Department of Finance, National University of Singapore (NUS). She is also an affiliated Research Fellow at the Wharton Financial Institution Centre and the Risk Management Institute, NUS. Her research covers comparative financial systems, institutions and mutual funds. She obtained her Ph.D. from the Boston College.

Saw Swee-Hock is Professorial Fellow at the Institute of Southeast Asian Studies and President's Honorary Professor of Statistics at the National University of Singapore. He is also an Honorary Fellow of the London School of Economics and Honorary Professor at the University of Hong Kong and Xiamen University. He is a member of the Board of Trustees of the National University of Singapore. His publications are mainly on statistics, demography and finance. Among his major publications are *ASEAN-China Economic Relations* (editor), *Managing the Economic Crisis in Southeast Asia* (editor), *Sovereign Wealth Funds* (co-author) and *Introduction to Islamic Finance* (co-author). He obtained his Ph.D. from the London School of Economics.

Shen Chung-Hua is Professor of Finance at the Department of Finance, National Taiwan University. He is a member of the President's Economic and Finance Advisory Committee and the Taiwan Resolution Trust Corporation Committee. He is also Director of the Board of the Taiwan Financial Holding Company, Taiwan Bank, Security and Futures Association and Taiwan Small and Medium Enterprise Guarantee Institute. His research interests are mainly in banking, financial markets, monetary policy, international finance and econometrics. He received his Ph.D. from the University of Washington.

Shin Jang-Sup is Associate Professor of Economics at the Department of Economics, National University of Singapore. His research interests include East Asian economic growth, financial crisis and restructuring, technology and innovation, and competitve strategies and organization of firms. Among his major publications are *The Five Theorems on the Financial Crisis and Policy Responses, Restructuring Korea Inc., A Paradigm Shift for the Korean Economy*. He has worked for about fourteen years in the Maeil Business Newspaper in Korea. He received his Ph.D. from the University of Cambridge.

Sarah Y. Tong is Assistant Professor of Economics at the Department of Economics, National University of Singapore (NUS) and a Research Fellow at the East Asian Institute, NUS. Prior to that, she held an academic position at the University of Hong Kong. Her research interests are in international trade, foreign direct investment, economic reforms and industrial restructuring. She obtained her Ph.D. from the University of California at San Diego.

John Wong is Professorial Fellow at the East Asian Institute, National University of Singapore. Until very recently, he was Research Director of the Institute. His main research interests are in the economy of China as well as the ASEAN economy. Among his major publications are *Understanding China's Socialist Economy, China's Emerging New Economy: The Internet and E-Commerce* (co-author), *China's Reform in Global Perspective* (co-editor), *Interpreting China's Development* (co-editor) and *Regional Economic Development in China* (co-editor). He obtained his Ph.D. from the University of London.

Naoyuki Yoshino is Professor of Economics at Keio University. He is also Director of the Financial Research and Training Centre at the Japan's Financial Services Agency. He serves as Chairperson of the Foreign Exchange Council and the Fiscal Council, Ministry of Finance, Japan. He was appointed Board Chair of the Financial Planning Standard

Board. He was conferred an Honorary Doctorate by the Goteborg University in Sweden. He obtained his Ph.D. from Johns Hopkins University.

Zhang Ming is Deputy Director at the Department of International Finance, Institute of World Economics and Politics, Chinese Academy of Social Sciences (CASS). His fields of interest include international finance, macro-economy, cross-border capital flow, and sovereign wealth management. Before joining CASS, he worked in KPMG and Asset Managers Group, a Japanese investment bank.

1

The Global Financial Crisis: Impact and Response in East Asia

Saw Swee-Hock and John Wong

The "Great Recession" and East Asian Economies

The global economy has barely recovered from the recent shock of the "Great Recession", which originated in the United States in 2008, first as the twin crisis of the subprime mortgage meltdown and the bursting of its housing bubble, and then quickly engulfed Wall Street to develop into the worst global economic crisis in decades.

The main causes of this financial crisis are now sufficiently well known. They include: (1) A long period of loose monetary policy, along with low interest rates in developed economies, generating too much easy liquidity to fuel excessive financial speculation activities; (2) Excessive "innovation" in the financial sector, leading to the proliferation of too many unsound financial products and too many complex financial instruments, for example, structured products such as CDOs (collective credit obligations) and derivatives such as CDSs (credit default swaps); (3) Deficient and inadequate regulations and supervision on banks and financial institutions, particularly the investment banks, e.g. many of their off-balance sheet activities; and (4) Failure of credit rating agencies in rating the many complex debt instruments correctly.

Meanwhile, as the global financial sector has basically recovered from the crisis, finance ministers, central bankers, and financial bureaucrats in the developed countries are busy debating and deliberating on a plethora of new policy measures to regulate the operations and practices of the financial sector in order to prevent the recurrence of similar crises in future. Many economists are also taking a critical look at the relevance and applicability of time-honoured economic theories such as rational expectation and the efficient market hypothesis that had been widely received and practised by financial economists and financial sector players.

When looking back, many economists have been greatly surprised not just by the rapid spread of the financial tsunami from one market to another, but by how rapidly the financial sector crisis had brought down the "real sectors" (production, exports, and employment) of the economy, that is, how the problems in "Wall Street" have been so quickly transmitted to "Main Street".

In the past, financial sector activities were a part of the "real economy" of production, consumption, and employment. In highly developed "post-industrial" countries today, financial services and financial activities have been growing much faster than manufacturing activities, particularly after the process of deregulation and globalization, starting with the liberalization of the London Stock Exchange (the so-called Big Bang) in 1986. Increasingly, financial sector performance is no longer closely correlated with "real" economic performance. Thus, Wall Street fortunes can go up and down, driven more by the influx of foreign capital and factors such as expectations and sentiments than real domestic economic changes in the United States. This is because the financial sector can usually grow on its own internal dynamics and resources, while "real sector" economic growth is determined by a different set of economic forces, such as technological progress and expansion of export markets. Hence, the Dow Jones index had been going through its boom and bust cycle without causing serious collateral damage to the real economy.

This time round, however, the situation has been significantly different. Partly due to excessive liquidity and cheap credit and partly because of the lack of adequate oversight, the financial sector had "overgrown" and "overexpanded". In particular, investment banks and non-bank financial institutions had overleveraged and overexposed themselves so much (Lehman Brothers on the eve of its collapse had leveraged itself over thirty times of its capital base) that they had created a systemic risk for the whole financial sector.

Wall Street banks used to derive most of their revenue from fee-based businesses such as M&A (merger and acquisition) advisory, equity and bond trading, debt underwriting, and assets management. Increasingly, however, young investment bankers considered these traditional banking activities "unglamorous". They were more inclined to take higher risks and higher leverage for a higher pay. Driven mostly by greed and the reward of large fees and subsequent big bonuses, practitioners of this form of what the Japanese used to call *zaiteki* ("financial engineering") had every incentive to create new products and find new ways to "make money with money", which led to overproduction of new financial instruments. And such complex new financial products could easily escape existing regulatory oversight through clever accounting such as hiding them under the "off-balance activities" of the banks.

Furthermore, these debt instruments were supposed to be properly screened and rated by the Wall Street's credit ratings agencies such as Moody's and Standard & Poor, which would grade the quality of the financial products in accordance with their degrees of risk exposure, and provide relevant information for the market to determine the "right" price for them. In this case, the ratings agencies had failed spectacularly in their job, as they treated the structured debt products much like a new class of corporate bonds, regardless of their risk profiles. Mis-rating of debt instruments led to their mis-pricing, which in turn led to over-risk-taking on the part of market players. Not surprisingly, a small spark of liquidity problem in one financial house easily created a rapid chain reaction for the whole financial sector to implode.

In the event, as U.S. banks, under mounting subprime mortgage pressures, started in the last quarter of 2008 to reduce their exposure to potential bad loans, and non-bank financial institutions started to unwind their debt positions, a severe credit crunch was created, with banks stopping to lend to one another and non-bank financial institutions scrambling for cover. Financial institutions had lost their mutual trust with one another to such an extent that a confidence crisis resulted, and this eventually led to the near collapse of Wall Street.

As major banks and financial institutions in Wall Street came to grief, normal banking activities were seriously disrupted, particularly in the credit market. Since credit is the "blood of trade", trade and investment were inevitably brought to a halt. Indeed, prior to the outbreak of the financial turmoil, the U.S. economy, severely affected by the collapse of the housing market and the resulting contraction of the building and construction industry, had started to slow down. In this way, the Wall Street crisis had deepened or aggravated, if not precipitated, the recession in Main Street.

But what about the economically dynamic East Asian region? Initially, many in East Asia were arguing that the U.S. economic crisis would not so easily and quickly spill over to the region. Granted, as financial activities everywhere are driven by sentiments and global capital movements, the U.S. financial crisis was expected to affect all financial markets the world over. Hence the old saying that whenever Wall Street sneezes, the world's financial markets will all catch a cold. However, it was thought that the contagion effect of the U.S. economic crisis on the "real economic sectors" in East Asia should be different. It had been argued that the strong economic fundamentals in most East Asian economies, plus a fairly high degree of intraregional trade (over 50 per cent of its total trade) in East Asia, operating as a strong regional engine of growth, would somehow "decouple" them from the adverse impact of the U.S. economic crisis.

As it actually turned out, many East Asian economies, including China as the most dynamic economy in the region, quickly succumbed to the global crisis, one after another with very little time lag. The plummeting of economic growth in Singapore and Hong Kong came as no big surprise, since both their financial sectors and real sectors were badly exposed to external fluctuations. But few would have anticipated that China's economy too should have fallen victim to the U.S. crisis so quickly.

Initially, as the global financial crisis was starting to unfold in Wall Street, many had expected that China's economy could somehow be "decoupled" from its adverse effect because its financial sector was basically insulated. But this had not actually been the case. In the event, the U.S. financial troubles quickly reverberated in China's export sector. The U.S. credit crunch almost instantaneously disrupted shipments of China's exports, and this, along with the expected drop in U.S. consumer confidence, created a chain reaction of pre-emptive cancellation of orders from Chinese factories, as well as the drying up of finance and credit for production, which led to widespread factory closures and massive retrenchments across the Pearl River Delta and elsewhere in China's coastal region. China's economic growth, therefore, started to plunge in the last quarter of 2009.

In fact, the global economy has become much more integrated and interdependent than we have realized, not just for financial sectors, but also "real economies". What actually happened this time was that the "real sectors" of East Asian economies suffered from this global crisis far more than their financial sectors, because East Asian economies are mostly outward looking in their orientation. Even for Hong Kong and Singapore, which are supposed to be the region's financial centres, the contagion effect of the U.S. financial crisis on their financial industry had been minimal.

Accordingly, most East Asian economies plunged into negative growth in the first half of 2009, with China's economic growth also plummeting to about 6 per cent. In response, most East Asian governments hurriedly put together various fiscal stimulus packages to prime the pump by boosting domestic demand (domestic investment and domestic consumption), with China's being the largest and most comprehensive.

Just as quickly as they were hit, most East Asian economies were by the turn of 2010 well on their way to recovery, with China's economy having rebounded most strongly, with 10 per cent growth in first quarter of 2010. According to the World Bank, "growth in the East Asia and Pacific region (particularly in China) as well as in South Asia (particularly India) has been resilient, buoyed by a massive fiscal stimulus package in China".[1] The World Bank has further forecast that the East Asia and Pacific region would continue to lead global recovery with 8.1 and 8.2 per cent growth in 2010 and 2011 respectively.

The way in which East Asian economies have bounced back so strongly and rapidly clearly underscores their strong economic fundamentals, particularly, their sound internal and external balances. It may therefore be argued that if the strong economic fundamentals of the East Asian economies had failed to "decouple" them from the global economic crisis, these had certainly provided a favourable precondition for their rapid economic recovery.

The main contributing factor for the region's rapid recovery came from the various fiscal stimulus packages and related policies adopted by individual East Asian governments. Thus, the experiences of the individual East Asian economies in managing their economic crises and coping with their economic problems should be of great interest to scholars and policy-makers.

A serious global economic crisis on such a scale is bound to bring about changes in global and regional geo-economic balances. In the aftermath of the "Great Recession", it is widely expected that global economic gravity will shift to East Asia. The East Asian experiences in coping with their economic crises should all the more hold valuable lessons for others.

A Glimpse of Various Countries' Experiences

Owing to the increasing importance of the Chinese economy (which has replaced Japan as the world's second largest economy), and as indeed China's economic growth has facilitated global and regional economic recovery, we have three chapters on China: Qian deals with the impact of the U.S. subprime crisis on China's financial system; Tong discusses how the global financial crisis affects China's trade development; and Zhang looks at the potential effect of the global financial crisis on China's swelling foreign exchange reserves.

Qian in her chapter starts off with a comprehensive review of China's financial sector development, along with the challenges and opportunities posed by the global financial crisis. Even though the global financial crisis had produced little direct impact on China's financial sector because of its relatively closed nature, China's real economy sectors had been badly affected. China's continuing efforts to reduce non-performing loans and improve banking efficiency, along with the overall improvement in the regulatory environment surrounding the operation of the financial markets, has certainly helped in preventing a stock market crash and a crisis in the real estate market. Capital controls have also prevented large-scale speculative capital movements that were the underlying cause for the 1997 Asian financial crisis. As a safeguard, China's policies towards improving the financial system had to be made along with supportive fiscal and trade policies.

Zhang's chapter focuses mainly on the impact of the global financial crisis on China's huge foreign exchange reserves, which increasingly look like a liability to China as the U.S. Government's rescue package potentially threatened the market value of U.S. treasury bonds and the U.S. dollar. To mitigate these risks, the Chinese Government adopted various remedy measures, including diversifying its foreign reserve assets, encouraging state-owned enterprises to invest more overseas, as well as promoting the greater internationalization of the Chinese yuan — China even mooted the idea of creating a supra-sovereign global reserve currency to replace the U.S. dollar.

Furthermore, Zhang stresses that these measures are not enough. For a fundamental solution to the problem, China's economy should speed up its domestic structural adjustment to reduce macroeconomic imbalances by promoting greater domestic consumption through increasing household income, providing more public social goods, opening up more service activities, and liberalizing commodity prices, interest rates, and exchange rates. Ultimately, the Chinese growth model should shift from being export- and investment-led to one that is driven more by domestic consumption. This would not only stabilize Chinese foreign exchange reserves, but also render Chinese economic growth more sustainable in the long run.

Tong examines China's trade prospects in the wake of the financial crisis. The global economic slowdown has brought about a sharp decline in China's exports, and with this, rising concerns over unemployment and social instability. Externally, China's gloomy export outlook also created an adverse chain reaction in the trade development of East Asian economies because of their growing trade interdependence. Their overall trade prospects could become even worse if the global financial crisis should cause these countries to modify the source of their economic growth from depending more on external demand to depending more on domestic demand, that is, more domestic investment and consumption, and less net export.

In the regional context, as Tong argues, East Asia (including Southeast Asia) should think seriously about taking bolder steps towards deeper and more comprehensive economic cooperation. Greater regional integration could become a new source of regional trade growth, which could also operate as a buffer against future external demand shocks emanating from outside the region.

As the region's most open economy, Hong Kong inevitably felt the immediate shock of the collapse of Lehman Brothers. Accordingly, both its stock market and housing market plunged. For the real economy, growth in the first quarter of 2009 also nosedived to −7.8 per cent. Overall, policy responses in largely *laissez-faire* Hong Kong appear to be less vigorous than in other East Asian economies. As Lui correctly points out, since Hong Kong has no central bank and the HK dollar is pegged to the U.S. dollar, employing monetary policies to deal with economic and financial crises was not a viable option. But the Hong Kong Government did put up a creditable counter-cyclical package comprising some infrastructure projects and employment creation policies. In the end, the Hong Kong economy quickly turned around, largely due to favourable economic spillovers from its hinterland — Mainland China.

In the chapter on Taiwan, Shen focuses on the role of Taiwan SMEG (bureau of Small and Medium Enterprise Guarantee Fund) as part of Taiwan's response to the financial crisis. SMEs are the mainstay of the Taiwan economy, especially important in terms of exports and employment. To counter the drastic drop in private fixed investment in this sector, the government introduced a "three-pillar" support policy in which it provided full deposit insurance for banks and addressed their liquidity needs; banks in turn extended loan periods for enterprises and raised the guaranteed coverage ratios for SMEs; and finally enterprises reduced layoffs and enforced no-pay leave for employees. To provide an immediate stimulus on domestic consumption, the government at the beginning of the economic crisis also tried out the innovative measure of issuing consumption vouchers to Taiwanese citizens.

The 1997 Asian financial crisis hit Korea primarily as a currency crisis, leading to a sharp depreciation of the Korean won and the rapid draining off of its foreign exchange reserves. Shin in his chapter on Korea shows that the global financial crisis this time again hit the won first. In the immediate aftermath of the collapse of the Lehman Brothers in September 2008, Korea suffered a sudden and massive capital outflow. This raises a number of critical questions regarding Korea's underlying exchange rate regime. The Korean economy had appeared on the surface as financially stable and having strong fundamentals, but the Korean won in recent years has actually depreciated much more than the currencies of East European countries. Shin suggests that Korea should discard the myth of having strong economic fundamentals and work instead towards reducing the discrepancy between market foreign exchange rates and that based on "fundamentals", by coming up with a system that can align foreign exchange rates with the real needs of the economy.

The Japanese economy experienced a decade of recession after the bursting of its asset bubble in the late 1980s, which brought down a total of 180 financial institutions. Since then property speculation has been very subdued and Japanese banks' exposure to complex financial instruments from outside has been limited. Yet, Japan, and also Germany, both strong economies in the developed world, were hit by the global financial crisis much more severely than others.

Yoshino's chapter starts off with the discussion of the Japanese bubble, and he further analyses the bubbles in China, South Korea, and the United States in light of the Japanese experience. For one thing, they all owed their origins to excess liquidity, and he strongly supports government use of Keynesian fiscal policies during a recession to stimulate domestic demand and revitalize economic growth by stepping up investment in infrastructure. But he thinks that in the process, some public works projects could well turn out to be wasteful and argues that the best way to prevent this from happening is for a government to make extensive use of private sector funds for public works projects. Private capital would naturally flow into projects that are profitable and hence ensure their long-term viability.

NOTE

1. See Chapter 1 of *Global Economic Prospects 2010*, 21 January 2010, available at <http://siteresources. worldbank.org/INTGEP2010/Resources/chapter-1.pdf>.

2
The Impact of the U.S. Subprime Crisis on China's Financial System

Qian Meijun

Introduction

The subprime crisis, which originated in the United States and shattered the global economy in 2008, offers valuable lessons on how a particular bank lending behaviour in one country, even a nation with high-level corporate governance practices and market regulation, can lead to a recession-generating collapse of the largest financial markets and several huge financial institutions. This chapter not only aims to understand the spreading mechanisms of the financial crisis and its effect on China's financial system, but also see what lessons China can learn and apply to its own financial system. What important issues does China have to cope with to maintain financial system stability in the future.

Since the Chinese financial system is relatively closed, the direct impact of the U.S. subprime crisis and the subsequent global financial crisis on China's financial system has been minimal, as was the case with the Asian financial crisis. However, the indirect impact through the real economy and government policies has been large and deep. Learning from the Asian financial crisis and Japan's prolonged economic recession, the Chinese Government has made a huge effort to reduce non-performing bank loans (NPLs), improve firms' corporate governance, and manage a controlled floating exchange rate for the RMB. The recent crisis offers new lessons for financial development, particular regulatory issues and the governance of financial institutions. If the Chinese Government takes proper measures and approaches to address issues related to these lessons, the crisis could actually offer China's financial system a major opportunity. That is, as long as government policy on foreign capital and institutional investors stays stable, we are likely to see an increase in financial capital investment, such as private equity and financial service industries, instead of the capital outflows typical for most emerging economies during any financial crisis.

This chapter addresses several issues that are important for the future development of China's financial system. First, investor protection is critical for stock market maturity, which in turn is critical for funding new industry. China therefore is provided with a golden opportunity to transform its industrial structure by developing technology-, capital-, and human capital-intensive industries. At present, this demand is met with supply, with large inflows of capital, technology, and talent. Therefore, China currently spends enormous amount of fiscal funds on encouraging new industry. However, as many lessons from other emerging countries show, this model frequently suffers from moral hazard and corruption problems. It can be more effective, however, if there is competition from the private sector, such as private equity funds. Second, China's bond market is still underdeveloped: the public corporate bond market is extremely small and corporate borrowing relies heavily on banks and informal lending channels, which significantly weakens the financial system's ability to deal with liquidity risk. One excellent example of such vulnerability is the rash of corporate defaults in early 2008 resulting from a temporary increase in interest rates. Such over-reliance on financial institutions makes their governance crucial. Improving investor protection and financial institution governance are therefore critical if China is to grab the opportunity arising from the financial crisis in developed countries.

Finally, the most significant challenge for China's financial system is to avoid damaging financial crises that can severely disrupt the economy and social stability. China needs to guard itself against traditional financial crises, including either a banking sector crisis stemming from possible accumulation of NPLs and a sudden drop in bank profits, or a crisis/crash resulting from speculative asset bubbles in the real estate market or stock market. China also needs to guard itself against new types of financial crises, such as the twin crises (simultaneous foreign exchange and banking/stock market crises) that struck many Asian economies in the late 1990s. Such a crisis is made more likely by large-scale and sudden capital flows and an increase in foreign speculation, a possible corollary to the introduction of cheap foreign capital and technology following China's entrance into the World Trade Organization (WTO). At the end of 2007, China's foreign currency reserves surpassed US$1.5 trillion, the largest in the world; by March 2008, they had increased to US$1.68 trillion. This rapid increase suggests the presence of a large amount of speculative "hot" money in China in anticipation of a continuing, and possibly considerable, appreciation of the RMB relative to other major currencies, especially the U.S. dollar. Thus, depending on how the government and the central bank handle the process of revaluation, there could be a classic currency crisis as they try to defend the partial currency peg. If such a crisis results in large withdrawals from banks, it could in turn trigger a banking crisis. Hence, before the world can accept the RMB as a viable currency for savings, an adequate balance is needed between capital control and the demand for free capital flows.

Overview of a Financial System

The financial system in any country typically consists of financial markets, such as the stock market, bond market, derivative market, and currency market; and financial intermediaries, such as commercial banks, investment banks, and assets management companies. Classified by transaction participants and the assets traded, a financial system comprises financial products such as loans, stock, bonds, treasuries, and mutual funds, and investors such as intermediaries, institutional investors, and insurance companies. It also includes regulators, such as central banks and stock or bank regulators, and is constrained by various rules and laws that govern transaction processes and participant rights and responsibilities.

A financial system's main function is to allocate funding. This function is carried out through either market pricing or intermediation and characterized by six important features: risk sharing, information acquisition, exercising corporate governance, company financing, supporting economic growth, and having the potential to spark a financial crisis. Whereas both markets and banks exhibit all these features, their ways of doing this differ dramatically (see Table 2.1). Essentially, a market is a direct financing channel through which funds reach fund borrowers directly; it therefore plays the role of facilitator. Fund transfer through banks, in contrast, is an indirect financing channel through which banks collect deposits from surpluses and then make loans to borrowers. Banks therefore not only facilitate transfers but also take on liability and an asset position in the process.

Fund transfers, however, also involve the transfer of risk, return, and information. Thus, because of their position differences, banks and markets also differ along the following dimensions. First, although banks intermediate risks by bearing the risk from borrowers and providing depositors with safe returns, markets only provide a possibility of risk diversification: the risks are fully borne by investors. Second, whereas banks play an active role in acquiring and evaluating borrower information, in the market company information is revealed through disclosure requirements or assets trading. Third, although both markets and banks are important governance forces, their governance mechanisms differ. Whereas banks can play a monitoring role and enter into negotiation with companies directly, market disciplining occurs through takeovers or investor exits that reflect on stock prices, which is likely to suffer from a "free rider" problem. Fourth, markets are better at providing funds to new industry, whereas banks are better at providing funding

**TABLE 2.1
Comparison of Market and Bank Features**

	Markets	*Banks*
Risk sharing	Diversification	Diversification and intermediation
Information acquisition	Disclosure and trading	Intermediation
Corporate governance	Market takeover, exit	Monitoring, negotiation
Financing firms	Mature firms and new industries	Mature firms
Supporting economic growth	Facilitation of direct investment	Indirect investment decisions
Financial crisis	Bubble and burst	Illiquidity and bad loans

to mature companies whose information is more easily accessed and assessed. Fifth, although both markets and banks provide financing that supports economic growth, markets do so by facilitating investor financing activities and providing a platform for investor pricing of company investments. Banks, on the other hand, provide financing by making lending decisions (choices in investment projects) for money from depositor pools. Finally, markets and banks differ in the type of crisis they engender. Crises arising from markets usually take the form of a bubble of asset pricing that bursts later on, whereas banks go into crisis when there is liquidity shock or accumulation of bad loans.

Impact of the U.S. Subprime Crisis

This section discusses how the recent U.S. subprime crisis and the global financial crisis it engendered have affected China's financial system and how it will affect its future development. An analysis of this dynamics suggests three main findings: (1) the direct impact of the crisis is minimal; (2) its indirect impact through the real economic sector is large; and (3) the government's reaction to the crisis, in terms of both economic policies and development policies for the financial system, will have significant and profound effects.

Contagion Channels

Although the subprime crisis originated in the United States, where home mortgages unaffordable by many mortgagees were securitized as investments, the contagious nature of modern economies means that a financial crisis in one country can eventually shake up the global economy. This contagion effect works through several channels. In the first, the capital market, financial institutions that are in trouble — particularly those holding troubled assets — are impacted when a loss in investment values produces a reduction in investment activities (for example, M&A [mergers and acquisitions], IPO [Initial Public Offering]) and stock prices fall accordingly. At the same time, a reduction in bank lending activities leads to liquidity shortfalls that make it difficult for firms to acquire financing, thereby engendering an economic recession. The second channel is the real economy itself: weak economic performance brings more pessimistic information to the markets, which results in further liquidity drops in the capital market. The third and fourth channels are financial market global integration and international trading. When parties involved in the banking and financial industries liquidate their investments in emerging countries, the constant and massive withdrawals affect liquidity in the financial markets of other countries. At the same time, amid alternating good and bad news, the rebalancing of risk portfolios causes large fluctuations in the price of equity. Hence, in this integration channel, economies characterized as financial hubs such as Singapore and Hong Kong will be most affected. Finally, real economic recessions spread to other countries through export and import and foreign investment, as well as through currency fluctuations.

Asian Financial Crisis as a Benchmark

During the 1997 Asian crisis, while its neighbouring countries went into recession, China remained stable due primarily to its insulated financial system in which most foreign investments are in real sector assets rather than financial assets, with capital controls in place. The contagion channel of stock market integration was therefore absent. In addition, China passed an economic stimulus package that supported continuing economic growth in the country. More significantly, China did not devaluate the RMB in response to the crisis, which also helped the recovery of neighbouring countries.

Yet despite the minimal impact, China learned three important lessons from the crash of other Asian economies and expanded tremendous efforts to prevent such crises from happening at home. First, it recognized the importance of capital control in a developing economy to reduce international liquidity risk and capital speculation. Second, it focused on reducing NPLs (non-performing loans) as the most important task in the banking industry for the next several years, thereby dramatically reducing the number of NPLs (see Figure 2.1). Finally, even though formal corporate governance mechanisms in China are still weak today, it has made great improvements in corporate governance compared with ten years ago, with attention and efforts paid by investors, firms, and regulators.

Particularly noteworthy is the reduction of NPLs through capital injection, asset purchases, and rehabilitation. To achieve such reduction, the Chinese Government first formed four state-owned assets management companies (AMCs), which, by offering debt-for-equity swaps, assumed and then liquidated the NPLs accumulated in each of the Big Four banks. This liquidation process included asset sales, tranching, securitization, and the resale of loans to investors.

FIGURE 2.1
NPL Balance and their Ratio in Major Commercial Banks, 2003–08

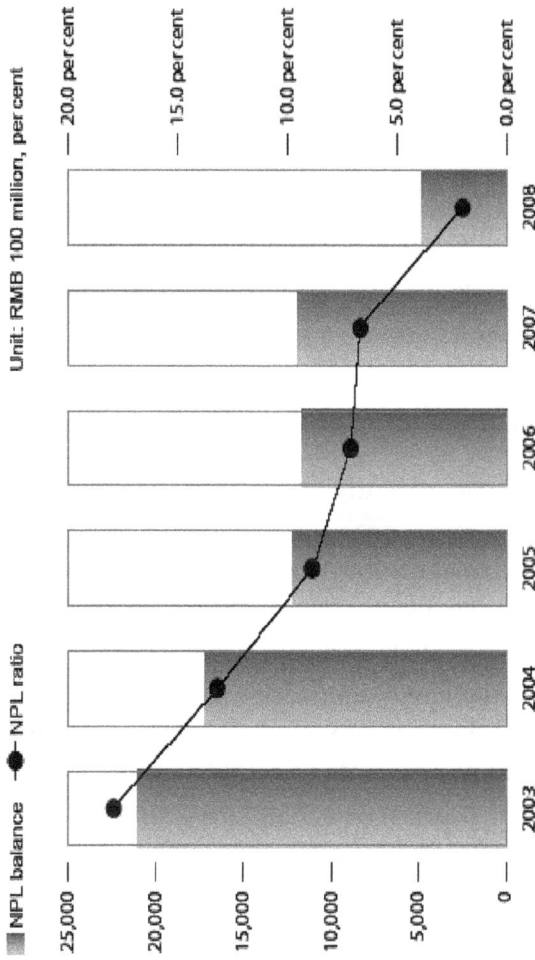

Source: China Banking Regulatory Commission, 2009 annual report.

Second, it injected foreign currency reserves, mostly in the form of U.S. dollars, treasury bills, euros, and yen, into these banks to improve their balance sheets and eventually push them into public listing. State-owned banks have also diversified and improved their loan structures by increasing consumer-related loans, while being more active in risk management and the monitoring of loans made to SOEs. The outline of NPLs in major commercial banks, depicted in Figure 2.1 shows how in both absolute amounts and ratio of total assets, NPLs dropped dramatically over ten years and by the end of 2008 were as low as 600 billion or 2.3 per cent of total assets.

Minimal Direct Impact on the Banking Sector

Although the recently increasing openness of China's financial system, especially in the banking industry, has made it more likely that China will be affected both directly and indirectly by economic crises elsewhere, compared with countries such as Japan, Korea, and Singapore, China is still relatively insulated. Not only is foreign ownership of Chinese banks relatively limited, but only a small portion of Chinese bank assets are in troubled U.S. assets — US$10 billion in U.S. structured credit products in all. In fact, only 3.7 per cent of the assets of the direct exposure of China's banking system had any direct exposure to subprime-related assets accounts (CBRC 2008). The value of risky bonds related to the collapse of Lehman Brothers also accounts for a low percentage of total assets. For example, whereas the disclosures of seven listed Chinese banks indicated holdings totalling about US$721 million worth of bonds related to Lehman Brothers and its subsidiaries, the US$70 million held by the Bank of Communication accounts for only about 0.02 per cent of its own total assets as of June 2008. Similarly, the Industrial and Commercial Bank of China (ICBC) held only US$152 million in bonds issued by or linked to failing or failed U.S. investment banks, while the Bank of China (BOC), which had lent Lehman subsidiaries US$53 million, held only US$76 million in Lehman Brothers bonds, close to the China Merchant Bank's (CMB) US$70 million. Given the size and profitability of these Chinese banks, the direct loss from the Lehman failure and other bankruptcies has had no major impact on their operations.

In fact, in contrast to the losses and bankruptcy of foreign banks, China's banking sector realized 583 billion yuan in after-tax net profits in 2008, up 30.6 per cent year-on-year. Likewise, its return on equity was 17.1 per cent, up 0.4 per cent year-on-year. Asset quality also increased: the provision coverage ratio for state-owned banks jumped to nearly 110 per cent in 2008 from 76.4 per cent a year earlier. Moreover, despite the crisis the amount of bad debt in Chinese banks fell sharply, with the sector's overall NPL ratio dropping to less than 2.5 per cent, down from 3.7 per cent the year before. This decrease, however, was mainly due to the writing off of 800 billion yuan (US$117 billion) in loans by the Agriculture Bank of China (ABC), the last state bank to receive a government bailout. Overall, however, as shown in Table 2.2, banks in China remained profitable in 2008 and showed healthy growth in various measures of profitability and asset quality.

TABLE 2.2
Performance of the Big Four Listed Commercial Banks at the end of 2008

Indicator	Item	ICBC	BOC	CCB	BOCom
Profitability	ROA	1.21	1	1.31	1.19
	ROE	19.39	13.72	20.68	20.86
	Cost Income Ratio	29.54	33.55	36.77	39.38
Asset Quality	NPL	2.29	2.65	2.21	1.92
Operational Prudence	CAR	13.06	13.43	12.16	13.47
	Large Exposure	2.90	3.40	3.68	3.81
	Provisioning	130.15	121.72	131.58	116.83

Notes: 1. Most data come from the annual reports of the commercial banks.
2. The provisioning of the BOCom was calculated by using impaired loans.
Source: China Banking Regulatory Commission, 2009 annual report.

Spuriously Large Direct Impact on the Markets

One really confusing observation, however, is that China's stock market was shaken hard by the crisis despite the small portion of its overseas qualified foreign institutional investors (QFIIs), and capital controls in the A-share market that were supposed to make China's stock market more insulated than its banking industry. The market dropped two-thirds of its capitalization before starting to recover, and as of December 2009, was only half of its peak value. This reduction may be related to the liquidity withdrawal mentioned above, although perhaps in informal or underground forms. Nonetheless, the direction of capital flows seems complicated and uncertain. For instance, in the first two quarters of 2008, China experienced a hot money inflow of about US$130 billion, even larger than that for the whole of 2007 (US$124.9 billion), while in the third and fourth quarters, it experienced a hot money outflow of about US$7.2 billion and US$90 billion, respectively (CRBC 2008).

This stock market collapse may perhaps be due to the sectors that are closely related to the U.S. economy, either in the investment or product markets. Other possible explanations are expectations, sentimentality, or a possible burst of the market bubble itself. As regards the latter, a comparison of the returns on a US$1-investment in the Shanghai Stock Exchange (SSE) index, the Singapore Straits Index (SSI), and S&P 500 shows that the SSE was sky-rocketing before the crisis surfaced. By October 2009, despite having dropped almost two thirds of its peak value two years previously, its relative performance was still higher compared with the STI and S&P 500 (see Figure 2.2). Hence, the bubble-and-burst explanation is reasonably convincing.

FIGURE 2.2
Comparison of Returns, 2006–09

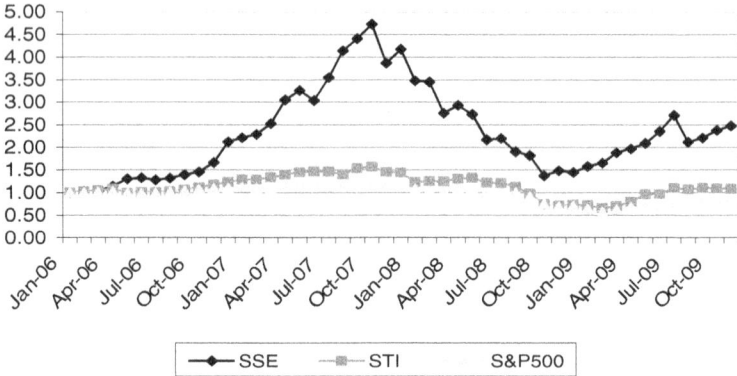

The bubble argument may not, however, be a sufficient explanation because China's stock market has performed poorly despite overall economic growth measured on a longer horizon. In fact, as Figure 2.3 illustrates, it has not only been highly volatile, but has also remained low on average until 2005 — even lower if compared with economic growth. In addition, stock trading in China is highly speculative as clearly shown by the very large turnover ratio and low concentration compared with most other major stocks worldwide (see Table 2.3). To illustrate, stocks on the Shanghai and Shenzhen Stock Exchanges, respectively, change hands almost twice and four times every year, compared with once or less in most mature stock markets. On the Shenzhen Stock Exchange, particularly, only one third of those trading are among the top 5 per cent large caps, implying an even higher turnover for average stocks. Finally, stock trading in China's stock markets reflects

FIGURE 2.3
Returns on Stock Indices around the World,
1992–2009

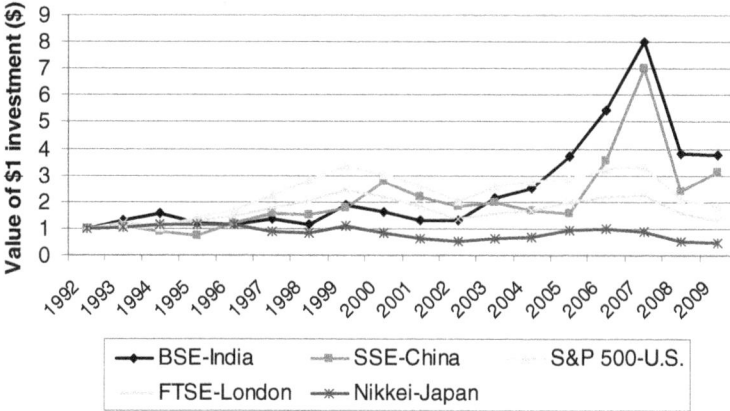

minimal company-specific information. As shown in Figure 2.4, 90 per cent of stocks tend to move up and down together compared with a ratio of near 50 per cent in other markets, which should indeed be the norm when bad and good company news arrive randomly (Morck, Yeung, and Yu 2000).

Indirect Impact Through the Real Economy

The banking system, as the economy's largest creditor, also depends on the real economy for earnings. For example, in late 2008 and early 2009, weak overseas demand, combined with interest rate fluctuations (reductions to defend economic growth and rises to curb the real estate bubble), led to a surge of defaults by export-oriented firms, especially small and medium-sized enterprises (SMEs). Admittedly, during

TABLE 2.3
Trading on Major Stock Exchanges, 2005

	Stock Exchange	Total Market Cap (US$ million)	Concentration (%)	Turnover Velocity (%)
1	NYSE group	15,650,832.5	57.2	167.1
2	Tokyo SE group	4,330,921.9	62.1	138.4
3	Euronext	4,222,679.8	68.1	136.9
4	Nasdaq	4,013,650.3	65.1	303.6
5	London SE	3,851,705.9	86.0	154.2
6	**Shanghai SE**	**3,694,348.0**	**73.6**	**211.0**
7	Hong Kong exchanges	2,654,416.1	74.4	94.1
8	TSX Group (Canada)	2,186,550.2	62.1	83.7
9	Deutsche Börse	2,105,197.8	78.5	208.4
10	Bombay SE	1,819,100.5	87.0	29.4
11	BME Spanish exchanges	1,799,834.0	—	191.9
12	National Stock Exchange India	1,660,096.9	68.5	67.7
13	Sao Paulo SE	1,369,711.3	65.7	57.1
14	Australian SE	1,298,315.0	87.4	101.6
15	Swiss Exchange	1,271,047.7	71.4	133.9
16	OMX Nordic Exchange	1,242,577.9	68.5	137.0
17	Korean Exchange	1,122,606.3	81.8	192.6
18	Borsaltaliana	1,072,534.7	66.5	204.1
19	JSE (South Africa)	828,185.3	33.8	52.5
20	**Shenzhen SE**	**784,518.6**	**38.7**	**389.2**

Notes: 1. Concentration = the fraction of total turnover of an exchange within a year based on the turnover of companies with the largest market capitalization (top 5 per cent)
2. Turnover Velocity = the total turnover for the year expressed as a percentage of the total market capitalization
Source: The website of the International Organization of Stock Exchanges, <http://www.world-exchanges.org>.

FIGURE 2.4
Information Content in Stock Trading

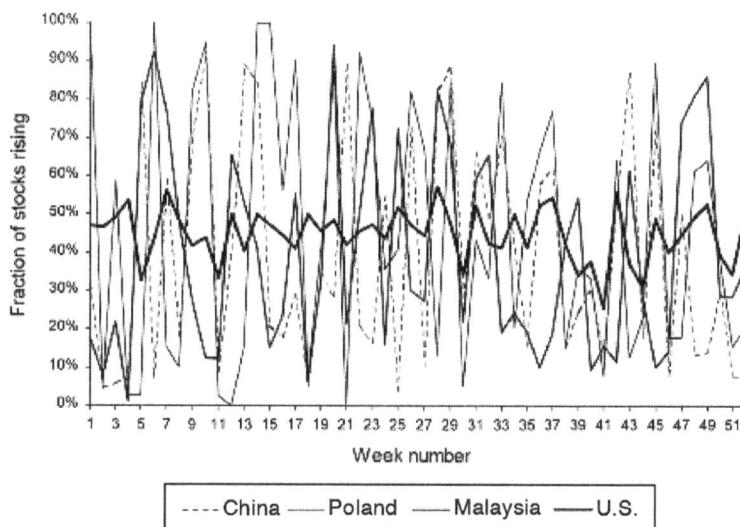

Note: Observed stock price synchronicity in the stock markets of selected countries. The fraction of stocks whose prices rise each week of 1995 in the stock markets of China, Malaysia, Poland and the United States based on returns including dividend income from Datastream.
Source: Morck, Yeung and Yu (2000).

this period, bank lending still showed some growth, but, reported against sliding profits, such growth might simply reflect a delay in the banking sector's response to the economic cycle: late 2009 reports anticipate increased NPL numbers. In addition, company and bank performances can affect foreign investors' market expectations, which in turn affect foreign direct investment and further impact the economy. For example, FDI, which was up 61 per cent in first quarter of 2008, had dropped 30 per cent by the year's end.

To deal with the economic shocks, China implemented a US$586-billion stimulus package, the largest ever, which covers housing, rural infrastructure, transportation, health and education, environment, new industry, disaster rebuilding, income, taxes, and financing. As long as the government takes the right measures to resolve crisis-related issues in a timely manner, crisis-imposed challenges will turn into opportunities. Likewise, as long as government policy on foreign capital and institutional investors stays stable, we can expect a booming of financial capital investment such as that in private equity and financial service industries. Nonetheless, China's financing of the US$700-billion bailout plan passed by the U.S. Government adds further pressure to the already unbalanced trading and capital accounts. The government may also use other policies instruments such as interest rates, but lower interest rates designed to spur investment may cause further bubbles in such financial markets as the stock and real estate markets.

Lessons to be Learned

The best benefits to any country from any crisis are the lessons learnt and the development of appropriate corrective measures. For instance, the Asian financial crisis motivated the Chinese Government to address its financial weakness; particularly, NPLs, overreliance on U.S. trade, and issues of corporate governance. As a result, great progress has been made in these areas in the past decade, with NPLs in the banking system dropping dramatically over time, thanks to the tremendous effort expanded. At the same time, international trade has become far more diversified, a board of directors system has been established, disclosure standards have been raised, and many firms have been delisted. In like manner, this new crisis offers many valuable lessons.

Regulatory Dilemma

The U.S. subprime crisis is forcing academics, practitioners, and policy-makers to consider several important issues. First, the government faces a regulatory dilemma, that is, given the critical role of financial intermediaries in the economy and governmental obligations to protect citizens' interests, the government must bail out intermediaries and markets that are troubled to avoid spreading a devastating situation throughout the whole economy. This obligation, however, causes a moral hazard problem: a financial intermediary — too large or too influential to fail — may expose itself to more risk than it can handle knowing that the country's citizens will bear the cost of any future government bailout.

This moral hazard problem can also be severe in Chinese banks. For example, although the Chinese Government has used foreign reserve assets to recapitalize state-owned banks with heavy NPLs, this injection plan does not prevent the banking system from originating new NPLs. In fact, it may create perverse incentives for state-owned banks that have received or will receive cash/asset injections if they believe that any future financial distress will again lead to a bailout. Such a belief replaces the incentive to improve efficiency with an incentive to take on risky projects. This moral hazard problem can thwart government efforts to keep NPLs in check. Such problems occurred in the United States during and after the 1980s government bailout of the S&L crisis (see, for example, Kane 1989, 2003). Hence, it is important for the government to make it clear that the injection plan is a one-time measure to boost banks' capital adequacy and these institutions can expect no future bailouts, especially after becoming listed companies.

Solutions to this moral hazard problem have occupied those in both government and academia for decades. Just as government ownership of financial institutions is not an ideal ownership structure, neither is a *de facto* government-backed private sector. Rather, allowing a two-way street of privatization and nationalization, with proper accompanying measures, can significantly reduce the moral hazard problem. Even within a strictly private sector, without our delving too deeply into the controversial issue of nationalization, "too big to fail" does not equal "too big to take over" or "too big to liquidate by steps". The essential issue here is a mechanism to ensure that it is the management, boards, and shareholders of financial institutions that take responsibility for their operations.

Governance of Financial Institutions

The market blames the U.S. subprime crisis on the fiduciary failure of many financial institutions. Specifically, at every stage of the subprime problem's formation, there seems to be an agency problem. First, during the U.S. real estate boom, lending standards dropped dramatically, and the use of automated loan approval allowed the authorization of many very risky loans without a proper reviewing process. Second, credit agencies paid by the investment banks and firms that structure and sell these products suffered from a conflict of interest. In the case of MBSs (mortgage-backed securities), there is speculation that investment grades were assigned to them based on risky subprime loans even though agents involved in the rating may have known that some rating processes were faulty. Finally, not only was incentive compensation for investment bankers focused on fees generated from assembling these financial products rather than product performance and profits generated over time, but the compensation for senior managers did not adequately factor in the increased risk taken by the banks.

Another growing problem for the U.S. market before the fall of the MBS markets was the weak governance of financial institutions, amply illustrated by the timing and late-trading mutual fund scandals of 2003 and 2004. In these cases, the management of funds with weak investor monitoring sold the right to arbitrage their shares to some hedge funds, and the arbitraging trading thereby diluted fund returns and hurt fund investor (shareholder) interests. China has also witnessed many scandals in both financial institutions and listed companies, in which certain financial institutions were complicit. Hence, governance in financial institutions is even more important for the health of financial markets than corporate governance. Whereas the failure of corporate governance may cause company bankruptcy and stock market inefficiency, the failure of governance in financial institutions can cause a crash of the entire financial system, and consequently the whole economy.

Nonetheless, to date the regulation of financial institutions, especially banks, has focused on such factors as their interest rate ceilings, operations, liquidity, and credit risk. Because in the traditional business model banks fundamentally take responsibility for their own transactions, including fund intermediation and its associated risks, little attention has been paid to agency problems. But the intermediation role changes significantly when loans are re-securitized, meaning that risks are simply repackaged and passed on to investors. Because of the lack of any governance mechanism related to this practice, investors rely largely on the reputation of banks and market self-discipline to ensure that banks fulfil their fiduciary duty in their intermediation of information and funds.

In Chinese firms also, although option-based incentive compensation contracts are not popular, the compensation schemes are far from simple. For example, CEO incentives may involve not only monetary pay-offs but also career stakes. Although the latter can lead to company inefficiencies, they can also provide incentives for top management to adopt long-term strategies. At the same time, reputation and relationships play a large role in China's business world (Allen, Qian, and Qian 2005). Hence, the governance improvements needed in China may lie in incentive setting, accountability mechanisms, and information disclosure.

Double-Edged Financial Innovation

Although financial derivatives can improve market efficiency by allowing pricing arbitrage, such arbitrage encourages speculation and gives rises to pricing complications when too many contingencies enter into the evaluation process. For example, properly estimating credit risk and the correlations among defaults is particularly important in MBS pricing. In fact, prior to the recent crisis, the initial underestimation of default correlation may have caused MBS overpricing, which was followed by post-default event overestimation that later caused underpricing and exaggerated the losses suffered by security holders. Furthermore, when the MBS originator and the funding providers are different, there is a lack of proper incentive aligning and disciplining, thereby making information production, and subsequently pricing, even more inaccurate.

In China, securitization also exists, but with much less pooling and repackaging. In a strict sense, intermediation takes the form of pure pass-through only, which, despite sharing some characteristics with repacking, has major differences. In terms of similarities, both involve the separation of originator and investor and therefore rely on a financial institution's fiduciary responsibility to control the risk passed on to investors. Unfortunately, however, there does not seem to be a ready mechanism to ensure that financial institutions are diligent in this duty once their role of information intermediary has disappeared from the securitization or pass-through process. As a result, safe practices must rely solely on reputation of the institutions and market self-regulation, which in turn increases the importance of interinstitutional competition and investor sophistication in financial innovation. Indeed, although no studies to date focus specifically on banking client sophistication and bank performance, Qian (2009) and Qian and Tanyeri (2009) show that investor sophistication is crucial if market discipline is to be effective in the mutual fund industry.

Alternatively, since securitization passes lender risk back to market investor, it is important that the mechanisms used are those typical in financial markets, such as disclosure requirements. Hence, those who are formulating bank regulations and security regulations in China — and any countries that have the securitization practice — may benefit from a cross-disciplinary collaboration to control risk in financial innovation by incorporating measures for adequate information disclosure for both institutions and markets.

Key Issues for Future Development

The recent U.S. subprime crisis has provided Asian countries, particularly China, with tremendous opportunities. First, large investment banks have begun to shift some of their business focus to the Asian region, meaning large capital inflows into the area and greater competition in its financial services industry. At the same time, the weakening of the U.S. economy has provided a golden opportunity for Asian countries to attract talent and technology, for example, the return of talent to China and India skyrocketed after the crisis. Likewise, the weakening of U.S. currency has challenged the U.S.-dominated global economic model. Whether China can take full advantage of these opportunities, therefore, depends on further development of its financial system, and to some degree, on political reform and social stability.

Currency

By September 2009, China's foreign reserves had reached $2.27 trillion, an amount that not only brings enormous risk, but also raises challenging questions on how to maintain its value, liquidity, and profitability, especially during the crisis period. As more than two thirds of its reserves are in the form of U.S. government bonds and loans, the U.S. economic recession posed a dilemma for the Chinese Government. On the one hand, the RMB faces tremendous appreciation pressure: the significant increase in foreign reserves is due partly to large sums of speculative foreign currencies in anticipation of the RMB appreciating relative to major international currencies, as well as a trade surplus and capital investment. On the other hand, an appreciation of the RMB means a loss of reserve values and the potential for capital outflow.

In fact, the lesson from Japan shows that a sudden appreciation in currency can have a devastating effect on a domestic economy, including a wave of bankruptcies among export-oriented firms, which in China are a major part of economic growth. Such large-scale bankruptcy can cause enormous pressure on bank liquidity and even solvency. If these problems are combined with a slowing economy, foreign capital may start to be withdrawn. Without some control over capital outflow, China could suffer the crisis typical in emerging countries due to sudden outward capital flows. Admittedly, however, since most foreign capital in China is in the real, and not the financial sector, the results may not be as devastating as those experienced by Asian countries during the Asian financial crisis.

Another dilemma related to China's foreign reserve is the large exposure to U.S. government bonds, which has forced China to bail out the U.S. currency despite a huge long-standing trade imbalance. It is therefore very important for China to diversify and slowly reduce its exposure to the U.S. currency. Yet in the third quarter of 2009, China's foreign reserves grew 6 per cent (a 24 per cent annual rate) due mostly to the purchase of U.S. treasury bills to bail the United States out of its economic crisis. Such growth and the reasons for it pose severe dangers down the road.

Risk Management

China's financial system, especially to banks, needs to improve prevention mechanisms for and management of the primary types of risk: interest rate risk, liquidity risk, credit risk, foreign exchange risk, trading risk, and counterparty risk. However, currently there is not only a lack of financial products for hedging against risk, but also a shortage of professionals skilled in internal risk control and external management. Nonetheless, even though foreign capital is limited to investment in China's financial securities, Chinese investors can access foreign financial products to meet the rising demand for risk hedging and investment diversification. Such access does not, however, address the lack of professionals versed in the derivative products that domestic investors can hold through foreign banks or domestic qualified financial institutions (DQII). Credit risk management is also made particularly hard by the virtual absence of any credit risk management system. State banks have taken a first step to resolving this problem, however, by developing a shareable database for managing the credit risk of commercial bank clients.

Another way of managing risk would be to supply more financial products so that investors can form diversified portfolios of more than just stocks. First, corporate bond markets should be developed, together with better enforcement of bankruptcy laws and regulation of bond rating agencies. Second, more derivative securities — such as forwards, futures, and options on commodities (already in place and trading), and other securities — should be introduced into the market so that investors and firms have more tools for risk management. Third, insurance companies should expand their coverage and offer more property and auto insurance products, as well as life and medical insurance. Nonetheless, as discussed earlier, any of these product developments would require an adequate assessment of their potentially harmful features, together with corresponding regulation and incentive compatibility design.

Funding New Industry/Investor Protection

The funding of new industry, which is better achieved by the market than banks, is important for China, especially at its current stage of wanting to develop more technology-, capital-, and human capital-intensive industries. The stock market in China, however, is unfortunately speculative and underperforming, which is problematic for its role in new industry funding. Even worse, despite the robust performance of the real economy, stock market performance has been volatile.

What deficiencies, then, underlie this problem? One possibility is the lack of alternative investment vehicles, which can also explain the current bubble in the real estate market. Another is the lack of inadequate investor protection, which must be improved if the stock market is to achieve the long-term efficiency necessary for China's successful transformation of industry.

On the other hand, the Chinese Government has endeavored to promote private equity investment to complement the weak venture investment from the private sector. However, as Lerner (2009) points out, government-run private equities worldwide mostly fail because of moral hazard, political goals, cronyism, and corruption. Likewise, the Chinese Government's expenditure of large amounts of fiscal money to fund new industry, while it may have resulted in some industry development, is very inefficient because of cronyism and corruption problems arising during the screening process and the lack of disciplining mechanisms to monitor those who obtain funding.

Crisis Prevention

Reducing the risk of a financial crisis in its financial system will be a critical task for China in the years to come. Although traditional financial crises may be triggered by NPL accumulation and a sudden drop in bank profits, more recent crises/crashes have resulted from speculative asset bubbles in the real estate or stock market. China must therefore guard against the twin crises of simultaneous foreign exchange and banking/stock market collapse which occurred in the Asian financial crisis of 1997.

The likelihood of such twin crises is increased by sudden and large-scale capital flows and foreign speculation. By September 2009, China's 2007 foreign currency reserve of US$1.5 trillion had risen to US$2.27 trillion, a significant part of which consisted of speculative money in anticipation of a continuing, and possibly considerable, appreciation of the RMB. The way in which the government and central bank handle the process of revaluation is therefore critical. Attempts to defend a partial currency peg, however, may trigger a banking crisis if there are large withdrawals from banks or a pulling out of foreign capital from other institutions, markets, or sectors. These risks not only concern when and to what extent a country should open its capital account and financial sector to foreign capital and foreign financial institutions, but also suggest that in China's current stage of financial development, capital control to a certain degree and a managed floating currency policy may be necessary for its financial stability.

Conclusion

After reviewing the different roles of financial institutions versus banks in a financial system, this chapter suggests that both markets and banks may have triggered the recent financial crisis, but in different ways. It also argues that the U.S. subprime financial crisis has impacted China's financial system less than that of some other countries, primarily because China's system, although quite open in some aspects, is relatively insulated. However, as explained in some detail, China's financial system still faces many developmental challenges both internally and externally and can learn valuable lessons from the U.S. subprime crisis. In fact, if policy-makers and practitioners in China can take proper measures, the impact of the crisis and the lessons learnt could provide China with major opportunities.

REFERENCES

Allen, Franklin, Jun Qian, and Meijun Qian. "Law, Finance, and Economic Growth in China". *Journal of Financial Economics* 77 (2005*a*): 57–116.

———. "China's Financial System: Past, Present, and Future". Wharton Financial Institutions Center Working Paper no. 05-17, 2005*b*.

China Banking Regulatory Commission. Annual Reports 2008, 2009.

Lerner, Josh. *The Boulevard of Broken Dreams: Why Public Efforts to Boost Entrepreneurship and Venture Capital Have Failed — and What to Do About It*. Princeton: Princeton University Press, 2009.

Kane, Edward. "Principal-Agent Problems in S&L Salvage". *Journal of Finance* 45 (1990): 755–64.

Kane, Edward, A. Hovakimian, and Luc Laeven. "How Country and Safety-Net Characteristics Affect Bank Risk-Shifting". *The Journal of Financial Services Research* 23 (2003): 177–204.

Morck, Randall, Bernard Yeung, and Wayne Yu. "The Information Content of Stock Markets: Why do Emerging Markets Have Synchronous Stock Price Movement?" *Journal of Financial Economics* 58 (2000): 215–60.

Qian, Meijun. "Is Voting with Feet an Effective Mutual Fund Governance Mechanism?" Working Paper, National University of Singapore, 2009.

Qian, Meijun and Basak A. Tanyeri. "Silent Runs in the Mutual Fund Industry". Working Paper, National University of Singapore, 2009.

Quarterly financial reports of Bank of China (BOC), the Construction Bank of China (CBC), the Industrial and Commercial Bank of China (ICBC), and Bank of Communication (BCOM).

The Statistical Bureau of China. *The Yearbook of China*, 2009.

Yahoo! Finance. "World Indices Returns, 1990–2008".

3
The Impact of the Global Financial Crisis on Chinese Foreign Exchange Reserves and China's Responses

Zhang Ming

Introduction

In many respects, the world is driven by major crises. The recent global financial crisis, which was triggered by the U.S. subprime mortgage crisis, is bound to bring dramatic changes to the world economic structure and international finance architecture. As a rising developing economy, China certainly could not escape the effects of the crisis. Its export-led development strategy is facing a serious challenge after the outbreak of the crisis. The shrinkage of external demand has led to the weak performance of Chinese's export growth, which hampers economic growth and labour employment. Because of income distribution inequality among sectors and inside households, as well as the underdevelopment of social public goods such as education, medical care, and a social safety net, household consumption is constrained at a very low level. Although the Chinese Government could ensure short-term economic growth by stimulating fixed asset investment, the fast growing investment will turn into much more serious excess capacity in the next three to five years not only in the manufacturing sector, but also in the infrastructure area, without the parallel growth of internal and external final demands. The enlarging excess capacity will result in a decline of profitability of Chinese corporations, a surge of non-performing loans on the balance sheet of Chinese commercial banks, and consequent deflationary pressure. If the Chinese Government does not make necessary structural readjustments to its old growth model in time, sustainable economic growth cannot be achieved.

This chapter will not focus on the real economy, but on the financial side of the story. Due to its export-led and FDI-led development strategies, China has accumulated huge foreign exchange reserves. While this may be a valuable national asset, it is also a reflection of tremendous resource misallocation that has led to twin surpluses of both China's capital and financial accounts. A large proportion of China's foreign exchange reserves is invested in U.S. dollar-denominated assets, especially U.S. treasury bonds. After the outbreak of the U.S. subprime crisis, the policy responses of the U.S. Government to stabilize its financial market and stimulate the macroeconomy have led to the deterioration of the U.S. fiscal deficit and the ballooning of debt on the Fed's balance sheet. It seems that the decline of the market value of U.S. treasury bonds and the significant depreciation of the U.S. dollar are unavoidable in the mid-term. If these developments really take place, the international purchasing power of the Chinese foreign exchange reserves will decline sharply. To mitigate the impact of the global financial crisis on the value of China's foreign exchange reserves, the Chinese Government has taken various measures, such as requiring the U.S. Government to behave more responsibly, speeding up the diversification of its reserve investment, encouraging state-owned enterprises to do more overseas investment, among other things. However, the potential risk of foreign exchange reserve devaluation cannot be eradicated, which is indeed a real cost of China's old growth paradigm. In the long term, the only effective way to ensure the security of China's foreign exchange reserves is to decrease the flow and further diversify the stock. To mitigate the accumulation of foreign exchange reserves, the Chinese Government should make structural adjustments as soon as possible, by changing its export-led growth strategy to a domestic consumption driven economic strategy.

Accumulation of Chinese Foreign Exchange Reserves

Entering the twenty-first century, China has seen its foreign exchange reserve growing rapidly (see Figure 3.1). While this stood at only US$165.6 billion at the end of 2000, it rose to US$1.95 trillion at the end of 2008, a tenfold increase. China has already surpassed Japan to become the largest foreign exchange reserve holder in the world. Because the Chinese Government has not fully opened its capital account, its foreign exchange reserve is indeed the major way for Chinese investors to hold overseas assets. For example, at the end of 2007, the total international assets held by the Chinese was US$2.29 trillion, of which Chinese foreign

FIGURE 3.1
Chinese Foreign Exchange Reserve, 1993–2008

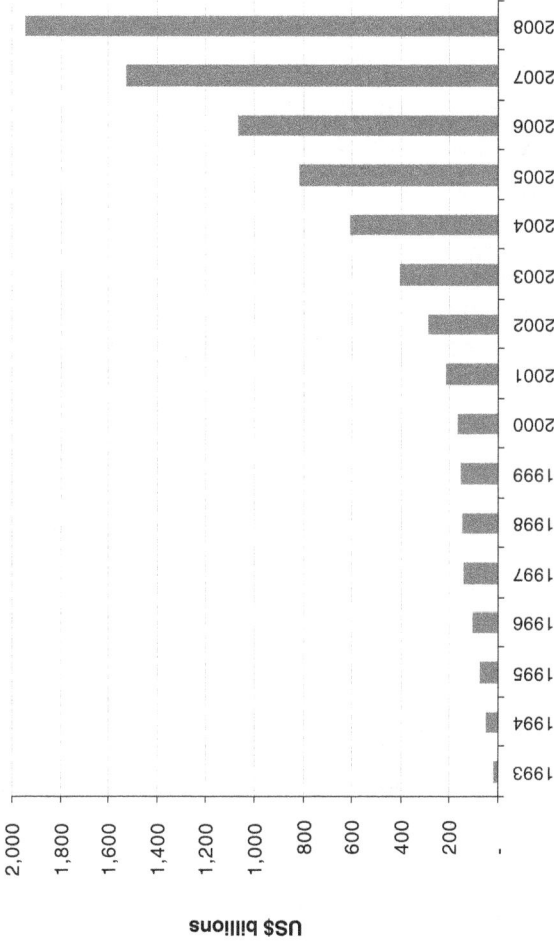

Source: State Administration of Foreign Exchange.

exchange reserve accounted for US$1.53 trillion, nearly 67
per cent of its total overseas assets.[1] The foreign exchange
reserve to GDP ratio hit 44 per cent in 2008.[2]

The Chinese Government has not disclosed either
currency composition or asset composition of its foreign
exchange reserves. We can only make a rough estimation
based on some related data sources. According to the
Currency Composition of Official Foreign Exchange
Reserves (COFER) figures released by the International
Monetary Fund (IMF), the currency composition of the
official foreign exchange reserves was as follows: U.S.
dollar-denominated assets, 60 per cent; euro assets, 31 per
cent; British pound assets, 5 per cent; Japanese yen assets,
2 per cent; and other currencies denominated assets, 2 per
cent. It is unfortunate that the Chinese Government does
not report its currency composition to the IMF. However,
we can assume that the currency composition of the Chinese
foreign exchange reserve is similar to that of other emerging
and developing countries. In other words, of the US$1.95
trillion foreign exchange reserve China had at the end of
2008, about US$1.17 trillion were invested in U.S. dollar
denominated assets.

The United States is China's most important overseas
portfolio investment market and the U.S. Government
releases data on foreign investments in U.S. securities
frequently. According to the U.S. treasury's Transactions of
International Capital (TIC) statistics, at the end of 30 June
2008, the investment portfolio of Chinese investors
(including both official and private investors) is as follows:
U.S. treasury bonds, US$535 billion (44 per cent of total
portfolio), U.S. agency bonds, US$544 billion (45 per cent),

U.S. corporate bonds, US$27 billion (2 per cent) and U.S. stocks, US$100 billion (8 per cent). Because China's foreign exchange reserves provide the major way for Chinese investors to hold overseas investments, and because most of the Chinese official assets are invested in U.S. dollar-denominated assets, we could use the above data to estimate the asset composition of China's foreign exchange reserves. The data demonstrate that most of Chinese foreign exchange reserves are invested in treasury bonds and agency bonds of developed countries, especially the United States.

The major force behind the fast accumulation of Chinese foreign exchange reserves are its continuous twin surpluses since 1999 (see Figure 3.2). China has been running a current account surplus since 1994, and its trade surplus is the main source of this current account surplus. From 1993 to 2008, China ran capital and financial account surpluses. An exception occurred in 1998 at the peak of the East Asian financial crisis. Inward foreign direct investments (FDI) are the major and relatively stable driver of capital and financial account surpluses.

Continuous twin surpluses are an abnormal phenomenon and a component of global imbalance. Theoretically, for a developing country which lacks capital and hence has more profitable investment opportunities, the ideal combination is a current account deficit and a capital account surplus. A developing country should use the capital lent from developed countries to buy machinery, technologies and manufacture of goods from abroad for domestic investment or consumption, that is, to translate its capital account surplus into a current account deficit (Willamson 1995). China has a continuous current account surplus, which means China's

FIGURE 3.2
Continuous Twin Surplus, 1993–2008

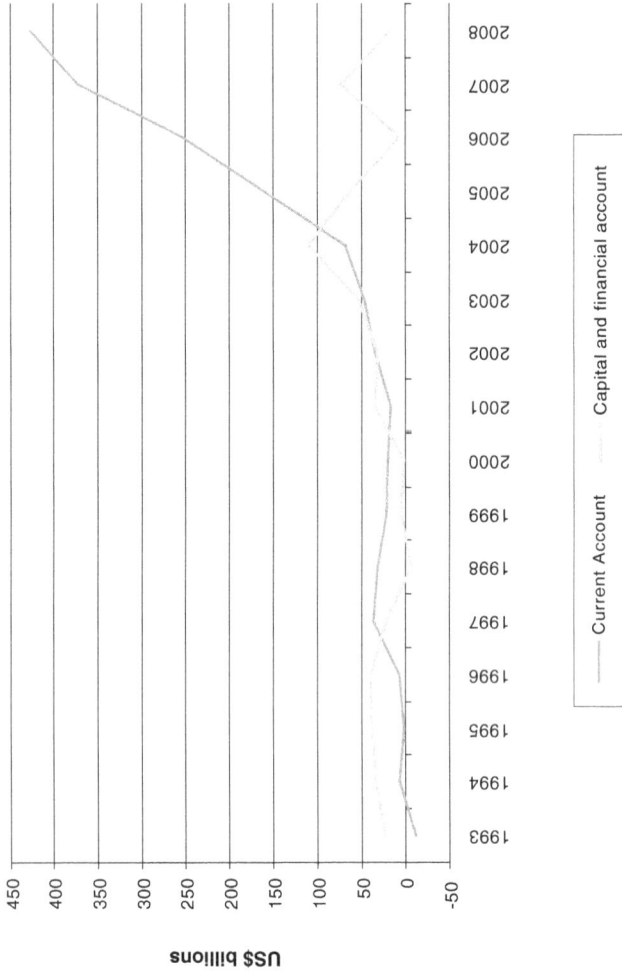

Source: State Administration of Foreign Exchange.

domestic savings is larger than its domestic investment. At the same time, China still has significant FDI inflows. Therefore, the twin surpluses of China reflect dramatic resource misallocations: on the one hand, it seems that China cannot translate its domestic savings into domestic investments; on the other hand, it seems that China cannot translate its FDI inflow into a current account deficit. The deep reasons behind this resource misallocation could be attributed to the underdevelopment of its domestic financial market, and its distorted policy incentives.

The classical explanations for the Chinese persistent current account surplus include a savings-investment gap, domestic and global economic cycles, and the global division of labour or global production network (Yu 2006). Beside these factors, the Chinese Government's export promotion policies play a critical role. To maintain the price competitiveness of Chinese exports in the international market, the Chinese Government has been intervening in the foreign exchange market to keep the RMB exchange rate significantly lower than its equilibrium level. Furthermore, the domestic price of unskilled labour, land, energies, and commodities are regulated by the government and kept at a low level. Therefore, the comparative advantage of Chinese exports is exaggerated by various distorted relative prices. The other side of enlarging trade surplus picture shows the generous subsidies Chinese households provide to consumers in advanced economies. It is ridiculous for poor Chinese households to provide significant subsidies to wealthy U.S. households. As regards the persistent FDI inflows, the Chinese Government's preference policies also play an important role. Because the scale of FDI utilization was introduced to the performance appraisal system for local officials, local governments introduce various preference policies to attract FDI, such as much lower corporate tax, cheap land, fiscal subsidies, etc. As a result of such distorted preference policies, some uncompetitive foreign enterprises entered China only for institutional arbitraging. Another consequence is the burgeoning of round-tripping FDI, that is, domestic capital which first flies away and then re-enters China in the form of FDI, with the objective of obtaining the policy preference offered by the Chinese Government. According to Xiao (2004), the Chinese round-tripping FDI to overall FDI ratio is about 40 per cent, which shows another example for resource misallocation.

As a result of these continuous twin surpluses, China has accumulated a huge inventory of foreign exchange reserves. Measured by any indicators such as import volume, short-term and maturing long-term foreign debt, and the need to intervene in the foreign exchange market, the size of China's foreign exchange reserves has already exceeded the optimum criterion. Consequently, the costs and risks of holding such a huge reserve are rising. First, the opportunity cost of holding foreign exchange reserves becomes more prominent. The Chinese Government invests a large proportion of its reserve in U.S. long-term treasury bonds, the yield of which is only 3 to 6 per cent. At the same time China receives significant FDI inflows every year, the stock of FDI at the end of 2007 reaching US$742.4 billion,[3] and the average annual ROI reaching 22 per cent![4] No doubt China has suffered great losses in this swap of domestic stocks with foreign bonds. Second, the potential U.S. dollar depreciation will cause the shrinkage of the international purchasing power of the Chinese foreign exchange reserves. Third, the accumulation of foreign exchange reserves has been causing the corresponding issuing of base money. Although PBOC could do sterilization through issuing central bank bills or raising the required reserve ratio, the sterilization is still incomplete and unsustainable. Therefore, the accumulation of foreign exchange reserves would lead to excess liquidity on the domestic market, which will cause asset price bubbles or inflationary pressure (Zhang and He 2009). The surge of Chinese stock and property prices from 2005 to 2008, and the inflationary pressure from 2007 to 2008, were all related to the massive accumulation of foreign exchange reserves at the same time.

Before the emergence of the subprime crisis, most academic literature covering a global financial imbalance concluded that a dramatic U.S. dollar depreciation will be the only solution to unravel a global imbalance (Roubini and Setser 2005), which will cause the decline of the international purchasing power of the Chinese foreign exchange reserves. However, the subprime crisis broke out in a totally different way. The initial loss made on subprime mortgage related financial products was amplified by high leverage, value at risk asset-liability management, and mark-to-market accounting methods. The bankruptcy of Lehman Brothers resulted in the collapse of the United States' Asset Backed Commercial Paper (ABCP) market, which caused the crash of the whole shadow banking system. The subprime crisis brought brand new financial risks for the value of the Chinese foreign exchange reserves. For example, in August and September 2008, Fannie Mae and Freddie Mac nearly went bankrupt. If this had happened, nearly US$400 billion of agency bonds held by the Chinese Government would turn into waste paper, which reached 10 per cent of China's GDP in 2008. As we will discuss in the next section, the U.S. Government's rescue package will have two major impact on the value of the Chinese foreign exchange reserves: the shrinking of the market value of U.S. treasury bonds, and the potential risk of the U.S. dollar's depreciation.

Rescue Package of the U.S. Government and Its Risk Implications

The U.S. subprime mortgage crisis broke out in the summer of 2007 as a result of the bursting of the real estate price bubble. The bankruptcy of Lehman Brothers elevated the U.S. subprime crisis into a global financial crisis. There were persistent liquidity squeezes and credit crunches on the U.S. financial markets. As the crisis spread from the financial markets to the real economy, the U.S. economy slipped into recession in the second half of 2008. To stabilize the financial market and stimulate the real economy, U.S. Government adopted unprecedented expansionary, systematic, and innovative macroeconomic policies (see Table 3.1).

Fiscal Policies and Risk Implications

As for fiscal policies, from February 2008 to February 2009, the U.S. Congress approved a US$168 billion Tax Rebate Act, a US$700 billion Financial Institution Recapitalization Act, and a US$787 billion Government Spending and Tax Rebate Act. The sum of the above three acts reached US$1.655 trillion, over 11 per cent of the U.S. GDP in 2008. Against the background of economic recession, the surge of fiscal expenditure would unavoidably result in the deterioration of the fiscal deficit. As Table 3.2 shows, the fiscal deficit in 2009 would reach US$1.84 trillion, and the total sum of the U.S. fiscal deficit from 2010 to 2019 is about US$7.1 trillion. The deficit to GDP ratio from 2009 to 2011 is much higher than the recognized sustainable level (3 per cent). And to make things worse, according to the U.S. Office of Management and Budget, the projected fiscal deficit from 2010 to 2019 should increase by US$2 trillion to reach US$9.05 trillion.[5]

The problem is how the U.S. Government is going to finance the fiscal deficit. Theoretically, it has three ways to finance the fiscal expenditure: raising tax, issuing treasury bonds, and printing money. During the economic recession, raising tax is not feasible. Printing money directly will cause inflationary pressure and asset price bubbles. Therefore, issuing more treasury bonds is the only practical way for the U.S. Government. As shown in Figure 3.3, from 1980 to 2007, the average annual US fiscal deficit is US$212 billion, and the average net issuance of treasury bonds is US$292 billion, which means that the issuing of treasury debt could mainly cover the fiscal deficit. However, the projected U.S. fiscal deficit reached US$1.84 trillion in 2009 and the projected net issuance of U.S. treasury debts in the same year would surpass US$2 trillion.

The question then is whether the demand for U.S. treasury bonds would match the surging supply. At the end of 2008, outstanding U.S. treasury bonds stood at US$10.7 trillion, of which U.S. Government entities held US$4.3

TABLE 3.1
U.S. Rescue Package

	Date	Content
		Fiscal Policy
Economic Stimulus Act of 2008	February 2008	US$168 billion income tax rebate
Emergency Economic Stabilization Act of 2008	October 2008	US$700 billion funding for Troubled Assets Relief Program (TARP) to recapitalize financial institutions
American Recovery and Reinvestment Act of 2009	February 2009	US$787 billion stimulus package for various spending and tax rebates
		Monetary Policy
Interest rate adjustment	September 2007 to December 2008	Lowered the target for Fed funds rate from 5.25 per cent to 0–0.25 per cent.
Term Auction Facility (TAF)	December 2008	The Fed auctions collateralized loans with terms of 28 and 84 days to depository institutions. Eligible collateral is the same as that accepted for discount window loans and includes a wide range of financial assets.
The Primary Dealer Credit Facility (PDCF)	March 2008	Eligible borrowers include primary dealers, and the term of loan is a repurchase

		agreement, whereby the broker dealer sells a security in exchange for funds through the Fed's discount window. The security acts as collateral.
The Commercial Paper Funding Facility (CPFF)	October 2008	To fund a special purpose vehicle (SPV) that will purchase three-month, unsecured and asset-backed commercial paper directly from eligible issuers.
Term Asset-Backed Securities Loan Facility (TALF)	November 2008 and March 2009	New York Fed will lend up to US$1 trillion (originally US$200 billion) on a non-recourse basis to holders of certain AAA-rated ABS, backed by newly and recently originated consumer and small business loans.
Purchasing agency bonds and treasury bonds directly	March 2009	The Fed will purchase up to an additional US$750 billion of agency (GSE) MBS, bringing its total purchases up to US$1.25 trillion, and will increase its purchases of agency debt by up to US$100 billion to a total of up to US$200 billion. Moreover, the Fed will purchase up to US$300 billion of longer-term Treasury securities in 2009.

Source: Wikipedia (Subprime Crisis; TAF; PDCF; CPFF; TALF).

Zhang Ming

TABLE 3.2
Projection of U.S. Fiscal Deficit, 2008–19

US$ billions, %

Year	2008	2009	2010	2011	2012	2013	2014	2015	2016	2017	2018	2019
Fiscal Deficit	459	1,841	1,258	929	557	512	536	528	645	675	688	779
Deficit GDP Ratio	3.2%	12.9%	8.5%	6.0%	3.4%	2.9%	2.9%	2.7%	3.2%	3.2%	3.1%	3.4%

Source: U.S. Office of Management and Budget.

FIGURE 3.3

U.S. Fiscal Deficit and Net Issuance of Treasury Bonds, 1980–2008

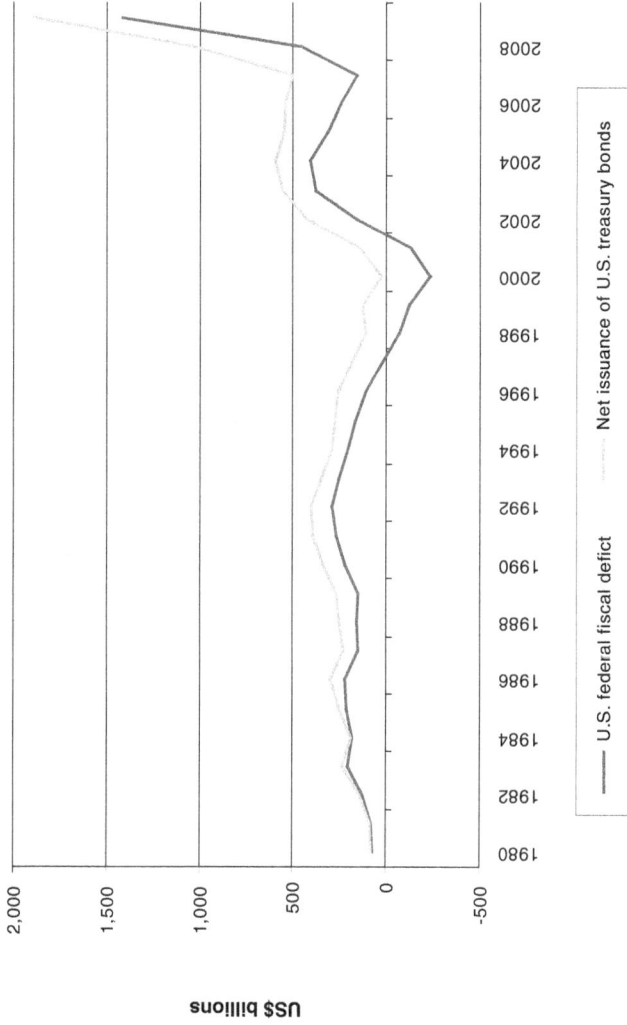

Source: U.S. Treasury, Bureau of Economic Analysis.

trillion (about 41 per cent), and the public held US$6.4 trillion (about 59 per cent). Of the public holding of U.S. treasury bonds, foreign investors held US$3.1 trillion. Simply put, 40 per cent of the potential demand for U.S. treasury bonds comes from U.S. Government entities, 30 per cent comes from foreign investors, and the remaining 30 per cent comes from U.S. domestic investors. We assume that U.S. Government entities could digest 40 per cent of the US$2 trillion U.S. treasury bonds issuance in 2009 again. Therefore, whether demand would match supply would depend on the demand from domestic and overseas investors.

Among overseas investors, the main demand came from East Asian central banks and sovereign investors from oil exporting countries. As developed countries slipped into recession, the global demand kept shrinking, so the demand for the export of East Asian countries was very weak, and the speed of foreign exchange reserve accumulation declined. Therefore, the incremental demand for U.S. treasury bonds from East Asian central banks became limited. The drop in oil price also caused the decline of oil exporting revenue, hence the incremental demand for U.S. treasury bonds from oil exporting countries also could not be counted on.

Of the domestic private investors, two main ones were financial institutions and households. During the period of deleveraging, the demand of financial institution for U.S. treasury bonds will increase because they are considered a safety heaven. However, when the deleveraging process is completed and financial institutions begin to allocate more risky asset, the demand for U.S. treasury bonds will decline. There is ample evidence that the deleveraging process of U.S. financial institutions was already completed in the first half of 2009. U.S. households lost a lot of wealth during the subprime crisis, so their new demand for U.S. treasury bonds cannot grow dramatically, even when we consider that the household saving rate has been rising significantly.

To summarize, we argue that the market demand for U.S. treasury bonds may not keep pace with the market supply in the next several years. The demand-supply gap will lead to a surging of the yields from newly issued U.S. treasury bonds, which will result in the decline of the market value of outstanding treasury bonds. Thus major holders of current U.S. treasury bonds will suffer a huge loss.

To curb the rise of new treasury bonds' yield and appease current major holders, the U.S. Government must fill up the demand-supply gap in the treasury bonds market. Therefore, it was reasonable for the Fed to announce in March 2009 that it would purchase US$300 billion long-term U.S. treasury bonds in 2009. This kind of quantitative easing did help to stabilize the treasury bond market. However it introduced new risks, that is, the risk of inflation and U.S. dollar depreciation.

Monetary Policies and Risk Implications

As shown in Table 3.1, from September 2007 to December 2008, the Fed funds rate had been cut from 5.25 per cent to 0–0.25 per cent. The scope for further interest rate cuts is very limited. Therefore, from December 2008 the Fed began to adopt new innovative policies measures such as TAF, PDCF, CPFF, and TALF, etc. The thrust of these quantitative easing measures was that the Fed injected liquidity directly into various financial institutions to mitigate the liquidity squeeze, and keep lending costs at a relative low level. Although these quantitative easing innovations made sense for stabilizing the short-term financing market, they also brought new risks.

The frequent use of quantitative easing measures resulted in the remarkable expansion of assets on the Fed's balance sheet (see Figure 3.4). The total assets of the Fed increased from US$800–900 billion before September 2008 to more than US$2.1 trillion in September 2009. Looking at the breakdown of assets, we found that it was the Fed's increased holding of liquidity and credit facilities (such as TAF, PDCF, and CPFF), and MBS which had caused the expansion of the Fed's total assets. At the end of September 2009, the ratio of liquidity and credit facilities and MBS to total assets reached 47.7 per cent compared with zero per cent two years ago, and the ratio of U.S. treasury securities holding by the Fed to its total assets decreased to 35.9 per cent compared with 87.2 per cent two years ago.

Why didn't the expansion of assets on the Fed's balance sheet since the outbreak of the global financial crisis cause any inflationary pressure till now? Analysing the Fed's balance sheet from the liability and capital side will help us find the answer. As Figure 3.5 shows, from September 2008 to September 2009, the increase in the Fed's total liabilities had been driven mainly by the deposits of depository institutions in the Fed. Because the financial market had been in great turbulence and the real economy had been very weak, commercial banks could not find enough profitable loan projects. Therefore they deposited a large proportion of funds in the Fed's reserve account. In other words, the injection of liquidity by the Fed did not lead to the growth of banking credit and broad money.

FIGURE 3.4
U.S. Fed's Balance Sheet: Supply Side, 2007–09

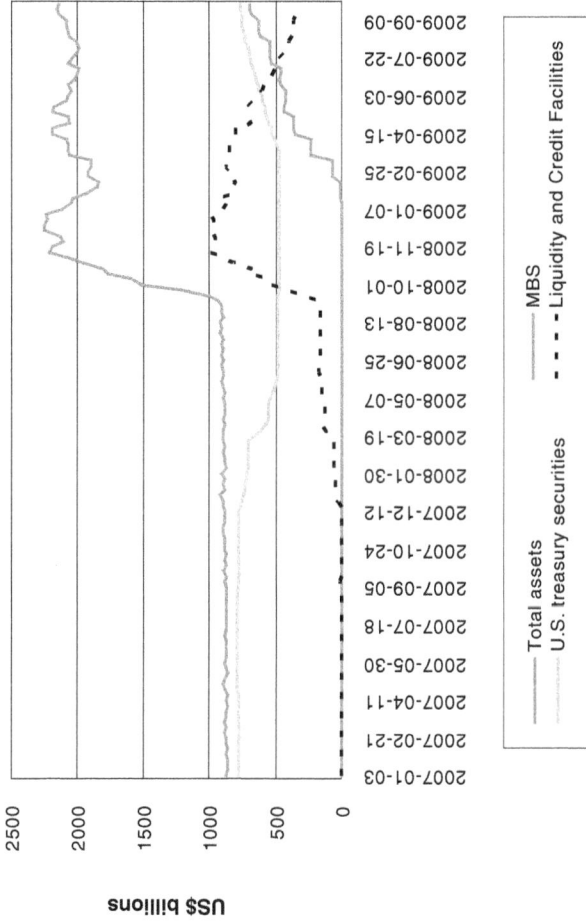

Source: U.S. Federal Reserve.

Zhang Ming

FIGURE 3.5

U.S. Fed's Balance Sheet: Liability Side, 2007–09

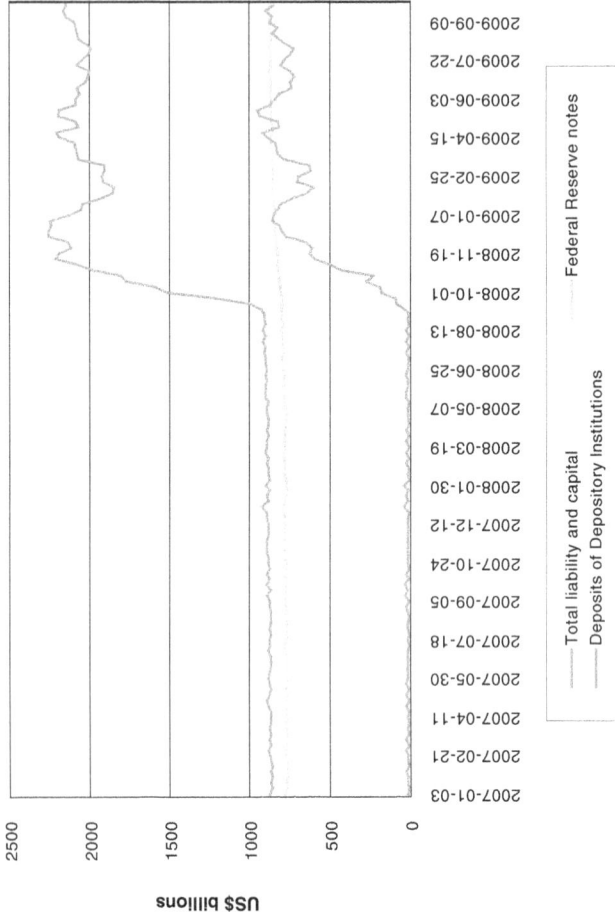

Source: U.S. Federal Reserve.

However, things could change very quickly. Once the financial market stabilizes, the deleveraging process of financial institutions will end, and the real economy will rebound. Commercial banks will decrease their deposits in the Fed and increase bank lending dramatically. With the growth of the monetary multiplier, the injected liquidity will translate into the rapid growth of banking credit. Therefore, inflation and a corresponding U.S. dollar depreciation will realistically become a menace.

U.S. Fed chairman Ben Bernanke was quite confident that the Fed could achieve a smooth exit from quantitative easing measures through raising the interest rate paid on reserve balances, using reverse repossession operations, issuing Federal bills, and selling assets directly.[6] However, none of the above exit strategies would be easy and cheap. For example, considering that a large proportion of assets held by the Fed are actually toxic assets purchased from troubled financial institutions, the Fed can only sell them by providing a large discount, which will incur a loss for the Fed. Issuing Fed bills and raising interest rate for reserve balances will both increase the Fed's expenditure significantly. Reverse repossession only postpones exit pressure. To summarize, these exit strategies would lead to losses for the Fed and exacerbate fiscal balance consequently. Therefore, it is difficult for the exit strategies to be executed smoothly without bringing new impact to the U.S. fiscal deficit or aggravating inflationary pressure. Furthermore, the Fed will bring on great pressure from Congress and the public if it executes its exit strategies in time because it risks killing the green shoots of economic recovery. However, if the Fed cannot exit from its quantitative easing measures in time, potential inflation and the related U.S. dollar depreciation will be unavoidable.

Chinese Government's Responses

As a result of its export-led development strategy, China has accumulated huge foreign exchange reserves. After the outbreak of the global financial crisis, the U.S. Government's rescue package is bringing new risks to the safety of the Chinese foreign exchange reserves because of the potential decline of the market value of U.S. treasury bonds and potential U.S. dollar depreciation. To mitigate the impact of the global financial crisis on the Chinese foreign exchange, the Chinese Government has taken fast and systematic countermeasures, which include criticizing U.S. policies directly, speeding up the diversification of its reserve assets, encouraging state-owned enterprises (SOEs) to make overseas investments, promoting RMB internationalization, and proposing a super-sovereign reserve currency.

Criticizing U.S. Policies Directly

In March 2009, Chinese Premier Wen Jiabao expressed his concern over China's U.S. treasury bonds in his annual press conference. "We have lent a huge amount of money to the U.S., so of course we are concerned about the safety of our assets. Frankly speaking, I do have some worries." Premier Wen then asked the U.S. Government to "maintain its credibility, honor its commitments and guarantee the security of Chinese assets".[7] This was the first time Chinese top leaders expressed their worries about the security of China's foreign exchange reserves.

While we do not think that Premier Wen's expression of concern and President Obama's rapid response on their own would strengthen the security of China's foreign exchange reserves, we still think that Premier Wen did the right thing. No one believes that China will sell a large proportion of its U.S. treasury bonds in the short-term because this will would harm China's own interest. However, as the largest holder of U.S. treasury bonds, China, through its statement, did exert some pressure on the U.S. Government's policies. Besides this, the diversification of foreign exchange reserve investments by emerging and developing countries is bringing a significant challenge to the U.S. dollar's status as a global reserve currency. To maintain the competitiveness of the U.S. dollar as an international reserve money and international investors' confidence in the U.S. dollar, the U.S. Government has to behave more responsibly and try to control its fiscal deficit and inflationary pressure to avoid any dramatic U.S. dollar depreciation.

Moreover, the Chinese Government's criticism of U.S. policies helped to increase its bargaining power in various bilateral negotiations. For example, whether the Chinese Government would continue to purchase U.S. treasury bonds has become a new weapon used by the Chinese delegation in several rounds of Strategic and Economic Dialogue between China and the United States. The balance reached by two sides might well be: China commits to continuing to buy U.S. treasury bonds and the United States commits to not to demand that the RMB appreciate against the U.S. dollar.

Speeding Up Diversification

In September 2007, the Chinese sovereign wealth fund named as China Investment Corporation (CIC) was established. The Chinese Government injected US$200 billion in foreign assets into CIC, making it one of the largest SWFs in the world. The major task of CIC is to acquire a more risky and diversified asset portfolio as compared with the conservative investment strategy of the State Administration of Foreign Exchange (SAFE). Between September 2007 and the fall of Lehman Brothers in September 2008, the investment portfolio of CIC was concentrated on financial institutions such as Black Stones and Morgan Stanley. The financial tsunami led to the crash of global stock prices, which resulted in significant losses for CIC. As a result of the criticism from the State Council and the public, CIC's investment strategy became more conservative after September 2008, and about 90 per cent of its investment portfolio was allocated in cash and cash equivalents. However, with the stabilization and rebounding of global financial markets, CIC became active again from the second quarter of 2009. The focus of CIC's new investment portfolio changed from the financial sector to natural resources and commodities. From January 2009 to September 2009, CIC invested US$10 billion in overseas mergers and acquisitions (M&A).[8]

The establishment of CIC introduced competitive pressure on SAFE in the management of the Chinese foreign exchange reserves (Eaton and Zhang 2009) and it began to modify its traditional investment strategy. In the past SAFE's portfolio focused on treasury bonds and agency bonds of advanced economies. After the establishment of CIC, SAFE expanded its investment in more risky assets such as corporate bonds and stocks. For example, according to figures disclosed by U.S. Treasury, from 30 June 2007 to 30 June 2008, U.S. corporate stocks held by Chinese investors rose from US$28.5 billion to US$99.5 billion, and it was believed that the main incremental investment came from SAFE (Setser 2009). SAFE also purchased some minority shares in dozens of U.K. or Australian listed companies through its subsidiary corporation in Hong Kong and London. After the outbreak of the global financial crisis in September 2008, SAFE suffered substantial losses from its aggressive investment in risky assets. Therefore, its investment style became more conservative again. In any case, after the crisis the diversification of China's foreign exchange reserves will continue not only in asset composition, but also in currency composition.

Encouraging SOEs to Make Overseas M&A

After the outbreak of the U.S. subprime crisis, global stock markets experienced a dramatic crash. The valuation of many companies' shares became more attractive compared with that pre-crisis. On the other hand, as a fast growing developing economy, China has become increasingly dependent on imported energy and commodities. Therefore, the Chinese Government has been promoting the overseas investment of SOEs since 2007, especially in energy and commodities. Overseas M&A by Chinese enterprises reached US$9.6, US$25.4, 50 and US$46 billion respectively from 2005 to 2009.[9]

Backing the overseas M&As of SOEs are Chinese policy banks which are responsible for providing relative loans, and the sources of foreign exchange loans come from China's foreign exchange reserves. In January 2008, the Aluminum Corporation of China (Chinalco) and the U.S. aluminum producer Alcoa bought a 12 per cent stake in the Britain-listed company Rio Tinto, an iron ore giant, at a cost of US$14.05 billion.[10] The direct objective of Chinalco's investment in Rio Tinto was to block BHP Billiton's merger with Rio Tinto. This merger would have strengthened the seller's monopoly in the iron ore industry, which will certainly hurt China's interest as it is the largest iron ore importer in the world. China Development Bank (CDB) played a critical role in providing M&A loans to support Chinalco's investment in Rio Tinto. It is necessary to mention that CDB received a US$20 billion capital injection from Central Huijin, a wholly-owned subsidiary of CIC. Looking at the above funding chain, we can understand how the Chinese Government is using its foreign exchange reserves to promote SOEs' overseas M&As. Although it is unfortunate that Rio Tinto rejected Chinalco's second bid of US$19.5 billion in June 2009, more and more Chinese SOEs have been successful in overseas M&As. For example, in April 2009 the Australian Government approved a revised US$850 million bid by Chinese Minmetals for mines owned by OZ minerals.[11]

Promoting RMB Internationalization

Before the global financial crisis, the process of RMB internationalization had been restrained by capital account controls, the RMB's inconvertibility and underdeveloped financial markets. Moreover, the incentive for the Chinese Government to promote RMB internationalization was not strong. However, after the outbreak of the global financial crisis, the Chinese Government, recognizing the potential risk of over relying on the U.S. dollar in its international trade and capital flow, changed its mind and became much more enthusiastic about internationalizing the RMB with the precondition of limited openness of its capital account (Zhang 2009).

From the end of 2008 till now, the People's Bank of China (PBOC) has signed bilateral local currency swaps worth a total of RMB 650 billion with Korea, Hong Kong, Malaysia, Belorussia, Indonesia, and Argentina. These bilateral local currency swaps are seen as a supporting mechanism for promoting the use of RMB in cross-border trade settlements. After the State Council executive meeting on 8 April 2009, the Chinese Government announced the first batch of cities for the RMB settlement experiment, which included Shanghai, Guangzhou, Shenzhen, Zhuhai, and Dongguan. In July 2009, the experiment of using RMB in cross-border trade settlements started. Moreover, the Chinese Government also issued 6 billion RMB-denominated treasury bonds in Hong Kong unprecedentedly in September 2009.

No doubt the Chinese Government will continue to promote RMB internationalization in the future, with the precondition of limited capital account openness. First, an offshore RMB settlement centre might be established in Hong Kong in the next couple of years, which could facilitate overseas investors to convert RMB with other currencies more freely. Second, an onshore or offshore RMB forward exchange rate market might be established in the future, which would help overseas investors to hedge off exchange rate risks while holding RMB positions. Third, more RMB-denominated financial assets which are issued by the Chinese Government, financial institutions, and corporations, will be provided in offshore financial centres such as Hong Kong. Fourth, an increasing number of foreign companies and financial institutions will be invited to issue RMB-denominated bonds or even stocks in the Chinese domestic financial market. However, before the RMB can develop into a real international currency, the capital account should be fully open and the RMB exchange rate should be determined by market forces.

Proposing a Supersovereign Reserve Currency

In March 2009, just before the London G20 summit, the governor of PBOC, Zhou Xiaochuan, published his article "Reflections on Reforming the International Monetary System" (Zhou 2009) in which he pointed out that the Triffin Dilemma could not be solved as long as one single national currency is used as a global reserve currency. This is because any country issuing the reserve currency cannot balance domestic monetary policy goals with the need to provide international liquidity. Therefore, a supersovereign reserve currency should be created to overcome persistent conflicts. This was the first time Chinese top leaders revealed their thoughts on the evolution of an international monetary system. Therefore it aroused great attention and feedback from the international community (Zhang 2009).

As it is very difficult to create a brand new super-sovereign reserve currency from scratch, Zhou suggested that the IMF's Special Drawing Rights (SDR) could be developed into a potential global reserve currency. Certainly, the Chinese Government's support for SDR would be based on certain conditions. First, the currency basket of SDR should be expanded to include more currencies of newly emerging countries such as the Chinese yuan and Indian rupiah. Second, SDR should be widely used in international trade and investment, such as private sector settlements, the denomination of commodity price, and foreign exchange reserves, etc. Third, the quantity of SDR should be enlarged and the distribution of SDR should be more equitable. Fourth, the governance of IMF should be improved to reflect the interests and voice of newly emerging countries and developing countries.

From the outbreak of the global financial crisis till now, the IMF's resources have been greatly strengthened, and China has played an important role in this. From August 2009 to September 2009, the IMF issued a total of US$283 billion worth of new SDR to member countries. In September 2009, the Chinese Government announced that it would purchase US$50 billion worth of SDR-denominated IMF bonds, and Brazil and Russia committed to the purchase of another US$10 billion. The Chinese Government was also interested in the creation of a Substitution Account inside the IMF, which means that member countries could deposit their extra U.S. dollar-denominated financial assets into an account of IMF and transform these into SDR-denominated assets.

Conclusion

As the result of continuous twin surpluses, China has accumulated huge foreign exchange reserves. The more than US$2 trillion reserves not only reflect serious resource misallocation, but also bring new costs and risks. After the outbreak of the global financial crisis, the U.S. Government's rescue package introduced two types of risks for the security of the Chinese foreign exchange reserves: the potential decline of the market value of U.S. treasury bonds and potential U.S. dollar depreciation. To mitigate the potential risks, the Chinese Government adopted prompt and systematic policy measures, including criticizing U.S. policies directly, speeding up diversification of its reserve assets, encouraging SOEs to make overseas M&As, promoting RMB internationalization, and proposing the establishment of a supersovereign global reserve currency.

Although the above countermeasures are necessary and effective, they are not enough. These solutions cannot eliminate all the risks which the Chinese foreign exchange reserves face. Realistically, the Chinese foreign exchange reserves will definitely suffer some losses in the future, and this is the inevitable cost China must pay for its traditional growth model. To solve the problem of its reserve security at its root, the Chinese Government should not only diversify its stock of foreign exchange reserves, but also decrease the future accumulation of foreign exchange reserves. It should speed up necessary structural adjustments, such as increasing household income, providing more social public goods, stimulating domestic consumption, opening up the service sector, liberalizing commodity prices, decreasing intervention on interest rates and exchange rates, and abolishing distorting preference policies towards export and FDI, etc. The transition of the Chinese growth model from being export and investment-led to being domestic consumption driven can not only stabilize Chinese foreign exchange reserves, but also promote the sustainable growth of the Chinese economy.

NOTES

1. The data are from Chinese international investment position statistics released by the State Administration of Foreign Exchange, China.
2. The GDP of China in 2008 reached 30.06 trillion RMB (Chinese Bureau of Statistics). The year-end exchange rate of USD against RMB is 6.829 (Bank of China). The calculation was made by the author.
3. The data are from Chinese international investment position statistics released by the State Administration of Foreign Exchange, China.
4. According to a World Bank investigation on 12,400 foreign enterprises in 120 cities of China, the average annual return on investment reached 22 per cent in 2005. The data are quoted from "World Bank: The Returns on Investment of Foreign Enterprises in China Reached 22 per cent" (in Chinese), *Xinhua Agency*, 11 November 2006.
5. "US Fiscal Deficit to Touch $9.05 Trillion in 10 yrs", *Business Standard*, 26 August 2009, available at <http://www.business-standard.com/india/news/us-fiscal-deficit-to-touch-905-trillion-in-10-yrs/07/24/71839/on>.
6. "Bernanke Outlines Fed's Exit Strategy", *Financial Times*, 21 July 2009.
7. "Wen Voices Concern Over China's U.S. Treasury", *The Wall Street Journal*, 13 March 2009.
8. "CIC Buys Stake in Kazakh Oil and Gas Group", *Financial Times*, 1 October 2009.

9. "China's Thirst for Mergers Barely Affected by Crisis", *Financial Times*, 31 December 2009.
10. "Chinalco, Alcoa Buy 12 Per Cent Stake of Rio Tinto's UK-listed Firm", *Xinhua Agency*, 1 February 2008.
11. "Update 2- Australia Approves New Minmetals-OZ Minerals Deal", *Reuters*, 23 April 2009.

REFERENCES

Eaton, Sarah and Zhang Ming. "A Principal-Agent Analysis of China's Sovereign Wealth System: Byzantine by Design". Research Center for International Finance, Working Paper no. 0910, Chinese Academy of Social Science, August 2009.

Roubini, Nouriel and Brad Setser. "Will the Bretton Woods 2 Regime Unravel Soon? The Risk of a Hard Landing in 2005–2006". Paper prepared for the Symposium on "Revived Bretton Woods System: A New Paradigm for Asian Development", organized by the Federal Reserve Bank of San Francisco and U.C. Berkley. San Francisco, 4 February 2005.

Setser, Brad. "SAFE Seems to Have Started Buying US Equities in the Spring of 2007 and Didn't Stop until July 2008", 15 March 2009. Available from <http://blogs.cfr.org/setster/2009/03/15>.

Willamson, John. "The Management of Capital Flow". Paper published in Pensamiento Iberoamericano, January–June 1995.

Xiao, Geng. "People's Republic of China's Round Tripping FDI: Scale, Causes and Implications". LAEBA Working Paper no. 24, December 2004.

Yu, Yongding. "Global Imbalance and China". Paper prepared for the Finch Lecture, Melbourne University, 17 October 2006.

Zhang, Ming. "China's New International Financial Strategy amid the Global Financial Crisis". *China & World Economy* 17, no. 5, September–October 2009.

Zhang, Ming and He Fan. "China's Sovereign Wealth Fund: Weakness and Challenges". *China & World Economy* 17, no. 1, January–February 2009.

Zhou, Xiaochuan. "Thoughts on Reforming International Monetary System", 23 March 2009. Available at <http://www.pbc.gov.cn/detail.asp?col=4200&id=279>.

4
The Global Financial Crisis and China's Trade Prospects

Sarah Y. Tong

Trade Expansion is Important for China's Growth

Trade expansion has been important, if not essential, for China's economic growth in recent decades. With an annual growth rate of 17 per cent since reforms started in 1978, trade has consistently outstripped the already staggering growth of the overall economy in which Gross Domestic Product (GDP) on average grew by 10 per cent a year. Consequently, China has become a leading trader in the world, ranking number two in export and number three in import in 2008, and accounting for 12 per cent and 9 per cent of the world total respectively. In 1978, China's trade to GDP ratio was about 10 per cent. It has since increased significantly, especially since the early 1990s, nearly doubling the 30 per cent in 1990 to reach 58 per cent in 2008.

More importantly, external demand has been an important engine for China's economic growth in recent years. Between 2005 and 2008, net export directly contributed about 20 per cent of China's annual economic growth (see Figure 4.1). Moreover, exports are crucial for developing China's industries and generating employment. In 2007, exports constituted about 25 per cent of China's total industrial output. According to the Ministry of Commerce, export related activities supported more than 100 million of those employed in 2008.[1]

In addition to providing market opportunities and generating employment, trade is an important source of productivity improvement, through economies of scale, competition, technology transfer, and the inflow of export-related foreign investment.

The importance of trade is also reflected by the negative drag over the past year on overall growth by a sharp decline in trade activities. Since late 2008, China's trade has suffered a sudden decline as a result of rapidly deteriorating external economic conditions generated by the global financial crisis. As export demand disappears, industrial output growth declines and overall GDP growth slows down.

Global Economic Downturn and the Sharp Decline of China's Trade

In 2008, a global financial crisis, triggered by the collapse of the housing market in the United States, began to spread to other sectors of the economy. The economies of the United States and the European Union, the world's two largest consumer markets, weakened considerably towards the end of the year, which led to a drastic decline in import demand.

According to the World Trade Organization (WTO), world merchandise exports grew by 1.5 per cent in 2008,

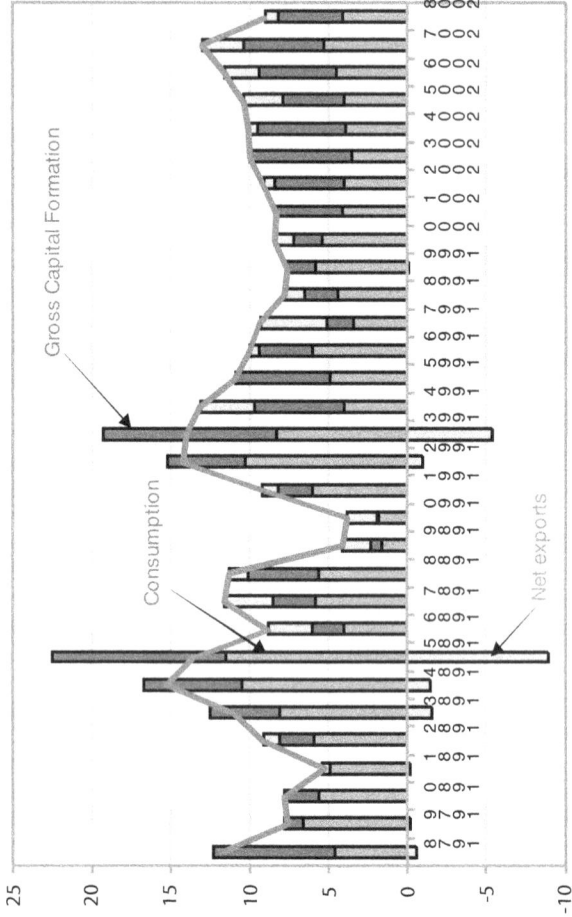

FIGURE 4.1
Sources of China's GDP Growth, 1978–2008

Source: China's Customs Statistics, various issues.

much lower than the 8.5 per cent in 2006 and the 6 per cent in 2007. This occurred alongside with the reduction of global GDP growth from 3.5 per cent in 2006 and 2007 to 1.5 per cent in 2008.[2] What is more significant, import by the world's major markets recorded negative growth in 2008. In the United States, European Union, and Japan, imports declined by 3.5 per cent, 1.5 per cent, and 2 per cent respectively in 2008, compared with positive growth of 1 per cent, 3.5 per cent, and 1.5 per cent respectively in 2007.

Towards the end of 2008, China's export trade began to experience a sharp decline, due mainly to the abrupt downturn in global demand for imports.[3] The first sign of a significant slowdown in China's trade came two months after the full eruption of the global financial crisis in September 2008. In November 2008, monthly export contracted by 2 per cent from that a year ago, compared with an annual growth of 19 per cent in October 2008. The change is even more drastic for imports, which contracted by 18 per cent in November 2008, a sharp fall from the 15 per cent increase in the previous month. The downward trend continued in the following months as falls in exports rapidly caught up with shrinking imports (see Figure 4.2). The most serious monthly decline occurred in January for import and February for export of 2009. When combined, the exports and imports of the two months contracted by 21 per cent and 34 per cent respectively as compared with the figures for the previous year. But the January 2009 trade statistics included an important seasonal element: the 2009 Chinese New Year was in late January while the previous lunar new year in 2008 was in early February. The statistics are thus more comparable when trade figures for January

FIGURE 4.2

China's Monthly Exports and Imports, 2008–09

(US$ billions and %)

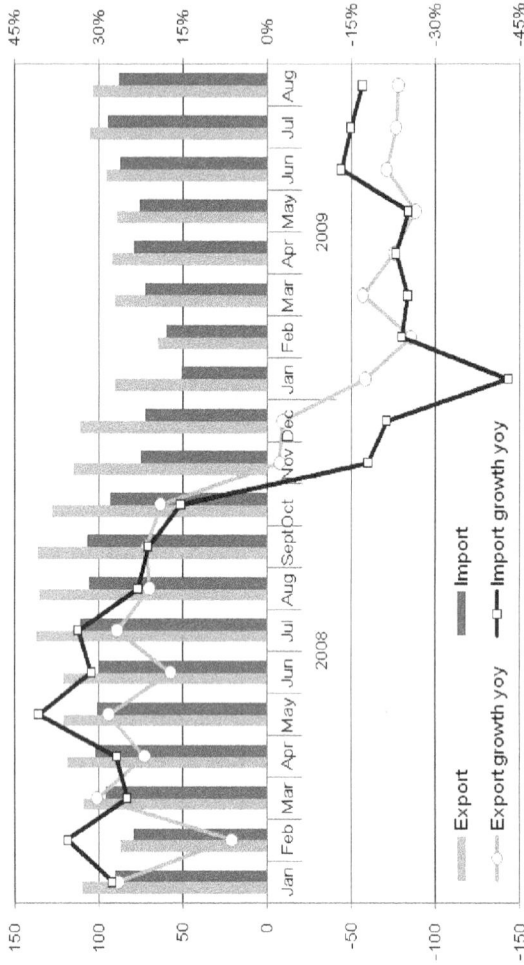

Source: China's Customs Statistics, various issues.

and February are combined. For the first quarter of 2009 as a whole, exports contracted by 20 per cent on a year-to-year basis, while imports declined by 31 per cent.[4]

Trade statistics since February seem to suggest a moderation in the rapid freefall as the contraction in trade has been modified, and the downward trend in monthly trade reversed. However, the prospect of a robust rebound in export remains uncertain. For each of the five months between April and August, exports were over 20 per cent lower than those of 2008. It is only in September when the contraction in monthly exports was narrowed to 15 per cent on a yearly basis. Meanwhile, import recovered more steadily than export. Between June and August in 2008, the decline in monthly import on a yearly basis was around 15 per cent. In September, import improved further to record the smallest reduction of 3.5 per cent compared with that of 2008. As a result, China's trade surplus has been moderated downward, and amounted to US$135 billion for the first three quarters, 26 per cent lower than that in the same period in 2008. This is equivalent to a monthly average of around US$15 billion for 2006.

The extent of the downward slide in China's trade has been both broad and deep. This is because over the past decade, China's trade expansion has been accompanied by closer economic ties with major economies in the world. China's rising trade with its Asian neighbours is of particular significance as the country has become the linchpin of an intensifying regional production network.

First, the economic recession in the industrial world, notably the United States and the European Union, led to a considerable fall in world trade through import decline. The

United States and the European Union are the two most important markets for China's export of finished products. Together, they account for about 40 per cent of China's total exports. The importance of the two markets for China's exports would be even higher if re-exports through places such as Hong Kong and Singapore are taken into account. According to China's official statistics, exports to Hong Kong accounted for 15 per cent to 20 per cent of China's total in recent years. Based on official statistics from Hong Kong, at least one third of re-exports originating in Mainland China was shipped to the United States and European Union. Consequently, we estimate an additional 5 per cent to 10 per cent of China's exports going to the two markets. Since 2002, after its accession to the WTO, China's trade with these two economies has expanded rapidly. Since late 2008, when the shock waves of the crisis spread from the financial sector to the real economy in the United States and the European Union, this upward trend has been reversed abruptly. Export to the European Union started to decline in December 2008 by 3.5 per cent on a yearly basis. The contraction worsened in the following months to 17.5 per cent in January, 30.2 per cent in February, and 20.2 per cent in March 2009. Comparatively, exports to the United States suffered slightly less and only began to decline in 2009, by 8.8 per cent in January, 24.2 per cent in February, and 12.3 per cent in March. In the first three quarters of 2009, the fall in exports to the United States and European Union was about 17.3 per cent and 25.1 per cent respectively as compared with that of the same period in 2008. It should be noted that exports to Hong Kong — of which a considerable portion is re-exported to the United States and the European Union, according to Hong Kong official statistics — also started to shrink in November 2008 before those to the United States and the European Union. Compared with those a year ago, the Mainland's exports to Hong Kong have decreased since November 2008. In the first three quarters of 2009, China's exports to Hong Kong declined by 21.7 per cent relative to the amount in 2008.

Within Asia, China's trade with Northeast and Southeast Asia both contracted, significantly more for imports. Between November 2008 and March 2009, China's total nominal export and imports contracted by 12 per cent and 26 per cent on a yearly basis. During the same period, exports to Japan declined by only 8 per cent while imports from Japan decreased by 24 per cent. The figures for Taiwan are 28 per cent and 49 per cent respectively. China-ASEAN trade was affected in much the same pattern; China's exports to ASEAN dropped by 15 per cent and imports by 32 per cent. Although part of the import decline is attributed to lower commodity prices due to slower global economic growth, this also reflects the serious chain reaction on the intense regional production network from a negative shock in external demand.

The heavy interdependence across Asia in trading activities is dominated by the purchase and sale of goods categorized as equipment and machinery in recent years, especially in transactions with China's major Asian trading partners. In 2008, for example, products under the broad category of machinery and appliances[5] made up more than half of China's total exports and 46 per cent of China's total imports, while items of traditional trade such as textile and clothing[6] accounted for only 15 per cent of total exports and 2 per cent of total imports.

Indeed, China trades heavily with its regional trading partners in machinery and appliances, especially for imports, which are, in large part, for processing and re-exporting to a third market. For example, machinery and appliances made up 43 per cent of China's export to, and 63 per cent of China's imports from, Japan in 2008. Similarly, the import of machinery and appliances from South Korea and Taiwan accounted for 60 per cent and 67 per cent respectively of China's total imports from these two economies in 2008. For ASEAN5 and Vietnam as a whole, China's import from this group of countries in machinery accounted for 58 per cent of its total in 2008.

Since late 2008, the export of such products was hit hard and started to underperform when compared with China's total exports. Between August and October 2008, the export of machinery and electronic appliances grew by 18 per cent, 18 per cent, and 15 per cent respectively, compared with that a year ago, while China's total export grew by 21 per cent, 21 per cent and 19 per cent in the same period. From November 2008, when total exports shrank for five consecutive months, the export of machinery and appliances continued to perform badly, contracting by 16 per cent on a yearly comparable basis, while total exports contracted by 12 per cent in the same period. Even more significant was the decline in the import of machinery and appliances — by 24 per cent in the five months between November 2008 and March 2009. Total imports shrank by 26 per cent due to a sharp contraction in the import of minerals, metals, and other materials, due in large part to falling commodity prices (see Figure 4.3).

Within China, firms in process trade were affected first and the most badly. As shown in Figure 4.4, while ordinary exports were still growing towards the end of 2008, albeit at a much lower pace, process trade started to fall in November 2008, by 11 per cent in export and 25 per cent in import. Ordinary imports also fell in November and December 2008, by 13 per cent and 16 per cent respectively. Into 2009, process trade continued to perform generally badly compared with ordinary trade, especially in imports.

Consequently, regions with a higher concentration of trade activities, especially of process trade, suffered more than the rest of China. The Pearl River Delta (PRD) region in Guangdong Province and, to a lesser extent, the Yangtze River Delta (YRD) region, are two such regions. As shown in Figure 4.5, as early as March 2008, export growth for the PRD region was already much weaker than for the rest of the country, while export growth for the YRD started to decline in the second half of 2008. The decline in imports of the two regions is even more dismal compared with the rest of the country (see Figure 4.6). Since January 2008, the monthly import growth for both regions has been considerably lower than for the rest of the country.

Overall, the global economic downturn has led to a sharp deterioration in world trade. As one of the world's top exporters, relying heavily on developed markets, China is hit directly and severely. Such negative external shocks spread far beyond China's borders to affect all major Asian economies, especially those that are more export-oriented. Intra-Asia trade, which has grown rapidly, to a large extent consists of intra-industry trade and is thus far from adequate to replace extra-regional demand. Therefore, the so-called decoupling between developing Asia and the developed economies in trade is still in its early development.

FIGURE 4.3
China's Monthly Export Growth, 2007–09 (%)

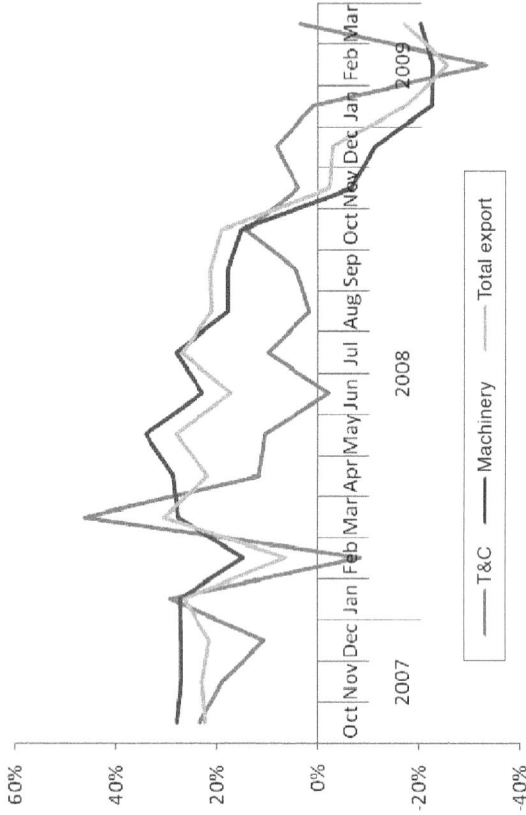

Source: China's Customs Statistics, various issues.

FIGURE 4.4
Monthly Growth of Ordinary and Process Trade, 2008–09

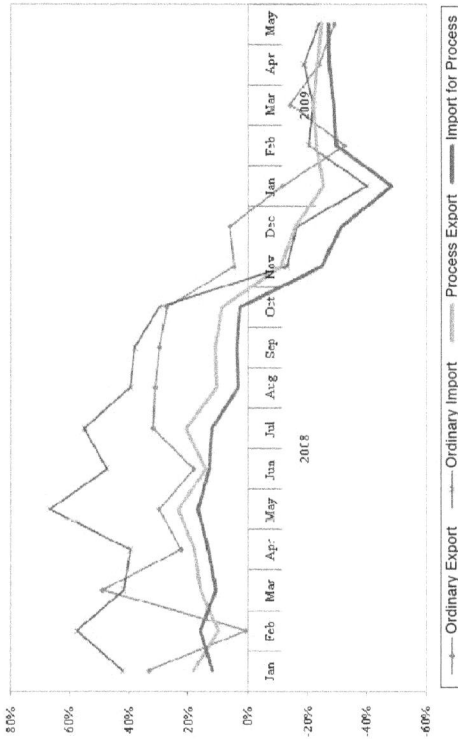

Source: China's Customs Statistics, various issues.

FIGURE 4.5
Monthly Growth of Exports for PRD, YRD, and the
Rest of the Country, 2008–09

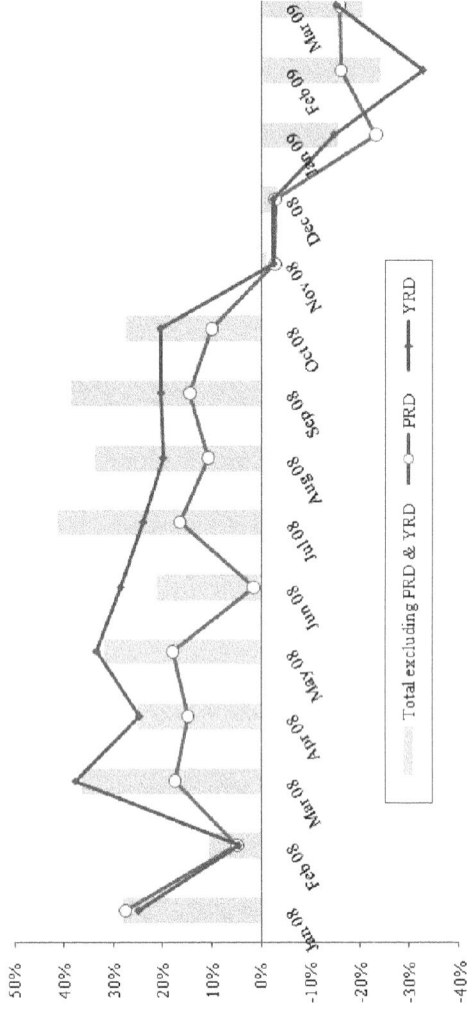

Source: China's Customs Statistics, various issues.

FIGURE 4.6
Monthly Growth of Imports for PRD, YRD, and the
Rest of the Country, 2008–09

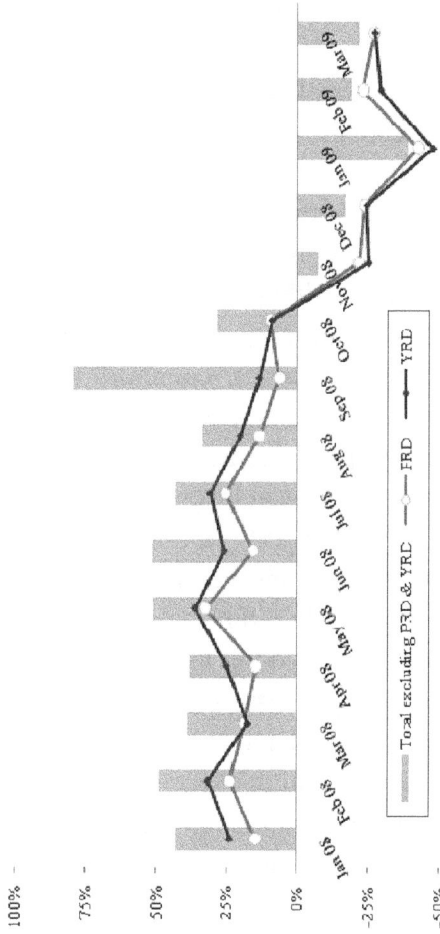

Source: China's Customs Statistics, various issues.

External Environment and Government Policy Measures

Faced with a worsening external environment, China's trade prospects in 2009 were clouded by gloomy expectations of continued decline. Indeed, the World Trade Organization predicted that global trade may decline by 8 per cent in 2009.[7] With recessions in the United States and the European Union still unfolding, the bulk of China's export was expected to fall further or stagnate. Trade between China and the developing markets is not immune to shocks from the economic crisis either, as demand from emerging markets constitutes only a small portion of global demand and the prospects for these emerging economies have also deteriorated.

To prevent further reduction in trade, and especially labour-intensive process trade, the Chinaese Government at both the central and local levels has promptly reoriented its economic policy towards boosting trade and controlling unemployment. Take the Pearl River Delta region, one of the worst hit areas in China, for example. The provincial government of Guangdong has pledged 200 million RMB in aid of export-process SMEs that are wading in dire financial straits.[8] Similarly, in the Yangtze River Delta region where there is also a high concentration of export activities, local governments, including those of Shanghai, Jiangsu, and Zhejiang, have met promptly and agreed to act in coordination to support export firms.

Almost immediately after the financial crisis made an impact on China's trade, especially on labour-intensive products, the Chinese Government adjusted upward tax rebates for these exports, which were lowered in September

2008 to encourage industrial upgrading. For the sectors worst hit, the government implemented two rounds of additional tax rebate and other measures to ease their difficulties with effect from November 2008 and April 2009. The first round of export tax rebate was targeted at labour-intensive goods such as textiles and some chemical products; the second round was introduced in accordance with the Key Industrial Development Strategy, covering mainly electronic appliances, chemical products, and textiles.[9]

An emerging concern for China's prospects in trade arises from potential trade conflicts and possible increases in protectionist measures. As the economic recession worldwide inevitably causes job losses and income decline, governments in both industrial and developing countries are under increasing pressure to resort to protectionism to safeguard the interests of their domestic industries. Although governments vowed not to raise trade barriers at the G20 meeting in November 2008 and again in early 2009, many have since either announced or implemented measures that are bound to obstruct trade, such as the well publicized *Buy American* clauses passed by the American legislature, although they were watered down somewhat in February 2009.[10]

Even before President Obama was sworn into office, there were growing worries that America might resort to protectionism to save domestic jobs. Indeed, since early 2009 there have been growing signs of protectionism in the United States, often in various obscure ways. On 10 March 2009, the American legislature passed a law which in effect forbids all Chinese exports of poultry and meat to the American market.[11]

In the late 2009, however, there seems to be an acceleration of protectionist moves in the United States. Between April and October 2009, the U.S. Department of Commerce has initiated twelve anti-dumping (or anti-dumping and countervailing) duty investigations on imports from China as compared with five during the same period in 2008, In fact, five were initiated in October 2009 alone.[12]

In September 2009, President Barack Obama signed an order to impose a 35 per cent tariff on Chinese-made tyre imports over the next three years, in response to a petition from the Steelworkers Union. On 30 October a U.S. trade panel approved the eighth government investigation in 2009 into charges of unfair pricing practices, alleging that Chinese producers receive government subsidies and sell at unfairly low prices in the United States. The U.S. companies want an almost 100 per cent duty or more on steel pipes imported from China. The Commerce Department was expected to make its preliminary decision on countervailing duties in December and on anti-dumping duties in February. On 6 November, the trade panel was to vote on three more investigations into Chinese pricing practices in separate cases on coated paper for high-quality print graphics, steel fasteners, and sodium and potassium phosphate salts. In 2009, the U.S. International Trade Commission (ITC) approved final anti-dumping or countervailing duties on nine Chinese products.[13]

The U.S.-China trade row manifests only the most dramatic development resulting from a rising global trend towards protectionism. Reports by the WTO and Global Trade Alert (GTA) warn that the G20 powers continued to implement protectionist measures, despite pledges in

Washington last November, repeated in London in April, not to do so. Besides the United States, other major economies have also heightened their protectionist measures.

According to the WTO, during the period 1 July–31 December 2008, the number of initiations of new anti-dumping investigations showed a 17 per cent increase as compared with the corresponding period in 2007. The number of new measures applied also increased between these periods. In particular, from July–December 2008, fifteen WTO members reported initiating a total of 120 new investigations as compared with 103 initiations reported by fourteen members in the corresponding period in 2007. As shown in Figure 4.7, there were 208 initiations of new anti-dumping investigations in the whole of 2008 as compared with 163 in 2007 and 202 in 2006.[14] China was the most frequent subject of the new investigations, with 34 new initiations directed at its exports.

A total of eleven members reported applying 81 new final anti-dumping measures in the second semester of 2008, 45 per cent higher than the 56 new measures reported by fourteen members for the corresponding period in 2007. These new final measures are the result of investigations initiated mainly in 2007 with length of time between initiation of investigation and applying final anti-dumping measure could be a year and a half.

On a yearly basis, there were 138 final anti-dumping measures in 2008 as compared with 107 in 2007 and 137 in 2006 (see Figure 4.8). Fifteen new investigations were initiated specifically by developed members, and 36 out of 81 new final measures were applied by developed members in the second half of 2008. This compares with 35 new

FIGURE 4.7
Anti-dumping: Number of Investigations Initiated, 1995–2008

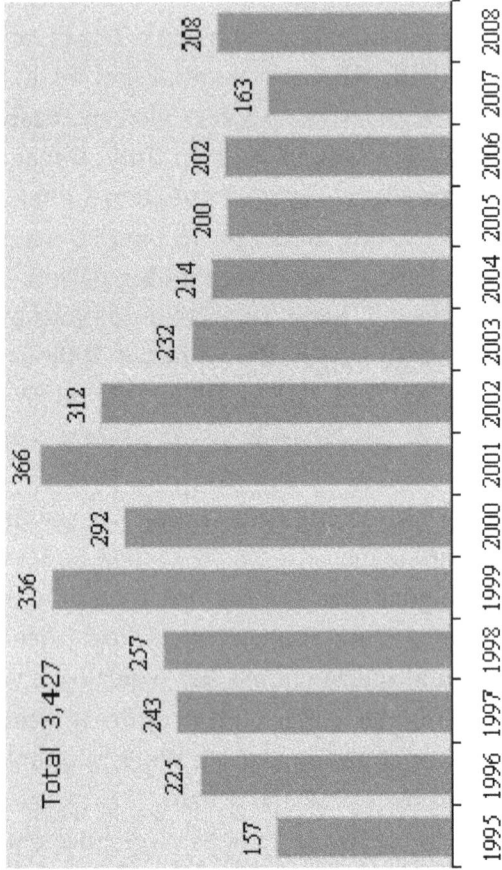

Source: China's Customs Statistics, various issues.

FIGURE 4.8

Anti-dumping: Number of Final Measures, 1995–2008

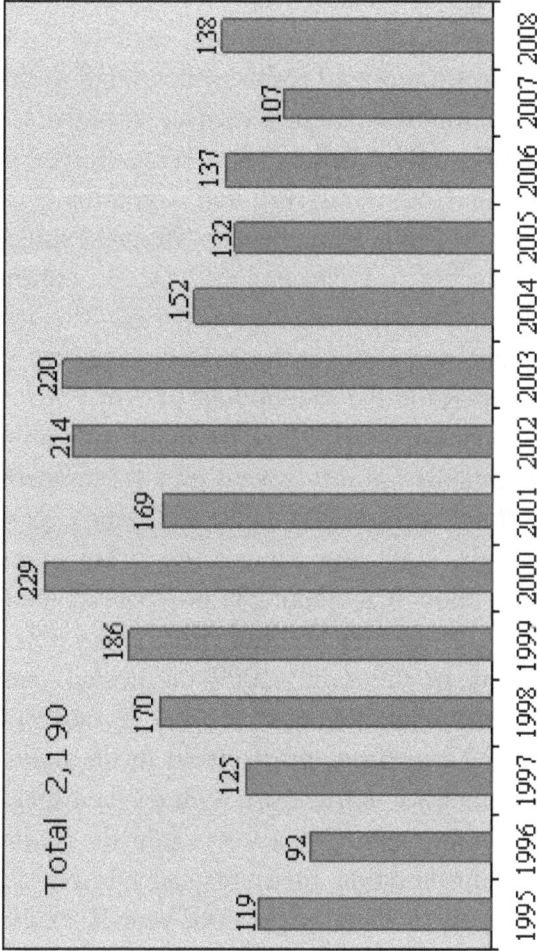

Total 2,190

Year	Number
1995	119
1996	92
1997	125
1998	170
1999	186
2000	229
2001	169
2002	214
2003	220
2004	152
2005	132
2006	137
2007	107
2008	138

Source: China's Customs Statistics, various issues.

investigations begun and 11 new measures applied by developed members in the second half of 2007.

As for the application of new final anti-dumping measures, the United States reported 21 new measures from July–December 2008, a significant increase over the two new measures it reported for the second half of 2007. India was second, reporting 13 new measures for the second half of 2008, followed by Turkey (11 new measures), Brazil (8), the European Community (6), and Argentina (3). Products exported from China were the most frequent subject of new measures during July–December 2008, accounting for 37 out of 81 new measures during this period. This represented a 42 per cent increase over the 26 new measures applied on Chinese exports in the second half of 2007.

In the year up to June 2009, the number of anti-dumping measures against unfairly priced imports jumped by more than one-third, according to the World Trade Organization.[15] Between July 2008 and June 2009, WTO members had notified the body of a total of 281 provisional and final anti-dumping measures they had launched. There were 201 such notifications in the same 2007–08 period. Among the members, the United States was the second most active user, with 47 measures, up from 30 in the previous year. India was the most active user, with 68 measures, up from 45 the previous year. China was again by far the biggest target of anti-dumping measures, accounting for 120 in 2008–09, up from 75 in the previous year. But China, which is often accused by its partners of being protectionist, cut the number of its notified measures to 14 from 18.

Facing a rise of protectionism in export markets, the Chinese Government has reiterated its willingness and commitment to support free trade and strengthen closer economic ties with its trading partners. Premier Wen Jiabao stated during his speech at Cambridge University in February 2009 that China would like to seek cooperation and mutual trust with all major world economies to combat the global economic recession.[16] This stance is reaffirmed by President Hu Jintao at the G20 summit held in early April through his own speech and the joint agreement in strong support of free trade and international coordination.[17]

At the same time, China has also begun to use various measures to protect its commercial interests. For example, on 27 September, China initiated anti-dumping and anti-subsidy investigations on imports of chicken products from the United States, following the U.S. decision to impose countervailing duty on imports of tyre from China. China also filed a complaint with the WTO against the U.S. decision on China's tyre export. On 12 October the Ministry of Commerce announced its final decision of the anti-dumping investigation on imports of Polyamide-6,6 from the United States, Italy, the United Kingdom, France, and Taiwan.[18] A week later, on 19 October China announced its preliminarily ruling on imports of Polycaprolactam (Polyamide-6) from the United States, the European Union, Russia, and Taiwan, and said it would start to collect preliminary anti-dumping duties in the range of 4 per cent to 36.2 per cent. In the following week on 23 October, China launched an anti-dumping investigation into imports of X-Ray Security Inspection Equipment from the European Union. On 1 November, for example, China's Ministry of Commerce announced the imposition of anti-dumping duties on imports of Adipic acid from the United States, the European Union, and Korea for a period of five year, ranging from 7.4 per cent to 35.4 per cent.

China's trade prospects in 2009 allowed no room for optimism. This is in part due to the overall gloomy prospect of the global economy. The International Monetary Fund (IMF) had estimated that the world's economic growth for 2009 would only be about 0.5 per cent and the growth rates for most advanced economies would be in the negative.[19] In addition, a recent report by the WTO estimates that world trade would decline by nine per cent in 2009, the biggest contraction since the Second World War.[20] Given such an environment, domestic measures to pursue further expansion in exports would be less than effective.

There is no doubt that downward pressure on the demand for China's export will in turn depress China's demand for imports, especially materials, parts, and equipment for process trade. Such a chain reaction will affect significantly trade relations between China and its regional trading partners, including those in Southeast Asia. Although intraregional trade within Asia has developed strongly over the past decade, much of this involves intraindustry trade which ultimately depends on the recovery in demand from the advanced markets.

What is more threatening is the acceleration of protectionist policies from industrial countries, as well as some developing countries, such as India. "The protectionist juggernaut shows no sign of slowing down", according to the latest report from *Global Trade Alert*, published by the Centre for Economic Policy Research, which also states: "Over 70 harmful measures have been enacted in each quarter of 2009, and almost every nation has been harmed by these measures." There are another 134 protectionist measures in the pipeline. This is equivalent to half a year's protectionism at current rates.

Over the past decades, China, as well as other economies in East and Southeast Asia, have relied heavily on export-oriented policies to achieve growth. With the current global economic downturn and heightened protectionist responses by major markets, it is time for policy adjustment. Domestically, countries may have to shift from investment-plus-export-driven growth to a more consumption-driven development, as their economies mature and their people become richer. In a regional context, East Asia and Southeast Asia should think seriously about taking bolder steps towards deeper and more comprehensive economic cooperation to facilitate economic integration. Given the size and the diversity of the region, it is possible to develop a stronger regional consumer market which would be the best buffer against external demand shocks.

NOTES

1. "Vice Minister Yi Xiaozhun of the Ministry of Commerce: China's Overall Economy Achieved Stable Development" (商务部副部长易小准: 商务运行整体平稳), 6 December 2008, <http://finance.sina.com.cn>.
2. World Trade Organization (WTO), "World Trade Developments in 2008", <http://www.wto.org>.
3. It should be noted that several domestic factors, such as rising labour cost and the reduction in the rate of export tax-rebate, also contributed to the weakening of China's export in 2008.

4. Trade data used in this chapter are mostly from *China's Custom Statistics* (various issues), unless specified otherwise.
5. These include products under Harmonized System (HS) Sections XVI (Machinery and Mechanical Appliances; Electrical Equipment; parts thereof sound recorders and reproducers, television image and sound recorders and reproducers, and parts and accessories of such articles), XVII (Vehicles, Aircraft, Vessels and Associated Transport Equipment), and XVIII (Optical, Photographic, Cinematographic Measuring, Checking, Precision, Medical or Surgical Instruments and Apparatus; Clocks and Watches; Musical Instruments; parts and Accessories thereof).
6. These include products under HS Sections XI (Textiles and Textile Articles) and XII (Footwear, Headgear, Umbrellas, Sun Umbrellas, Walking Sticks, Seat Sticks, Whips, Riding Crops and parts thereof; prepared Feathers and Articles made therewith; Artificial Flowers; Articles of Human Hair).
7. World Trade Organization (WTO), 2009 press releases, "WTO Sees 9 per cent Global Trade Decline in 2009 as Recession Strikes", 23 March 2009, <http://www.wto.org/english/news_e/pres09_e/pr554_e.htm>.
8. <http://www.fibre2fashion.com/news/textile-news/newsdetails.aspx?news_id=66796>.
9. Ministry of Finance, People's Republic of China, "Announcement on Raising the Rate of Tax Rebate for Export of Labor-intensive Goods" (关于提高劳动密集型产品等商品增值税出口退税率的通知), 17 November 2008, <http://szs.mof.gov.cn>.
10. David E. Sanger, "Senate Agrees to Dilute 'Buy America' Provisions", *New York Times*, 4 February 2009, <http://www.nytimes.com>.

11. "China Blasts 'Discriminative' U.S. Measure on Chinese Poultry Imports", *Xinhua News Agency*, 13 March 2009, <http://news.xinhuanet.com>.

12. International Trade Administration, U.S. Department of Commerce, "Press Releases 2006–2009", <http://trade.gov/press/press_releases.asp>.

13. They include mattress inner springs, small diameter graphite electrodes, welded stainless steel pipes, steel threaded rods, front-seating service valves, circular welded carbon quality steel line pipes, critic acid, tow-behind lawn groomers, and kitchen appliance, shelving, and racks. The investigation approved covers seamless carbon and alloy steel standard, line and pressure pipes used in industrial piping systems to convey water, steam, oil products, natural gas, and other liquids and gases.

14. World Trade Organization (WTO), 2009 press releases, "WTO Secretariat Reports Increase in New Anti-dumping Investigations", 7 May 2009.

15. *Business World*, "Antidumping Measures up in Year to June", 2 November 2009, <http://beta.bworldonline.com/main/content.php?id=723>.

16. "Full Text of Chinese Premier's Speech at University of Cambridge", *Xinhua News Agency*, 3 February 2009, <http://news.xinhuanet.com>.

17. "Hu Jintao: To Promote the Diversification and the Rationalization of the International Monetary System" (胡锦涛: 促进国际货币体系多元化合理), *China Daily,* 3 April 2009, <http://www2.chinadaily.com.cn>; "A List of the Main Outcome of G20 Summit in London" (G20伦敦峰会主要成果一览), 2 April 2009, *China News Service*, <http://news.sina.com>.

18. From 13 October 2009, anti-dumping duties ranging from

5.3 per cent to 37.4 per cent will be levied on import of Polyamide-6,6 from the United States, Italy, the United Kingdom, France, and Taiwan.
19. "IMF Expects G-7 Growth to Grind to a Halt", *New York Times*, 8 February 2009, <http://www.iht.com>.
20. "WTO Sees 9 Per Cent Global Trade Decline in 2009 as Recession Strikes", WTO, 23 March 2009, <http://www.wto.org/english/news_e/pres09_e/pr554_e.htm>.

REFERENCES

"A List of the Main Outcome of G20 Summit in London" (G20伦敦峰会主要成果一览). *China News Service*, 2 April 2009. <http://news.sina.com>.

"Antidumping Measures up in Year to June". *Business World*, 2 November 2009. <http://beta.bworldonline.com/main/content.php?id=723>.

"China Blasts 'Discriminative' U.S. Measure on Chinese Poultry Imports". *Xinhua News Agency*, 13 March 2009. <http://news.xinhuanet.com>.

"Full Text of Chinese Premier's Speech at University of Cambridge". *Xinhua News Agency*, 3 February 2009. <http://news.xinhuanet.com>.

"Hu Jintao: To Promote the Diversification and the Rationalization of the International Monetary System" (胡锦涛：促进国际货币体系多元化合理). *China Daily*, 3 April 2009. <http://www2.chinadaily.com.cn>.

"IMF Expects G-7 Growth to Grind to a Halt". *New York Times*, 8 February 2009. <http://www.iht.com>.

International Trade Administration, U.S. Department of Commerce. "Press Releases 2006–2009". <http://trade.gov/press/press_releases.asp>.

Ministry of Finance, People's Republic of China. "Announcement on Raising the Rate of Tax Rebate for Export of Labor-intensive Goods" (关于提高劳动密集型产品等商品增值税率的通知), 17 November 2008. <http://szs.mof.gov.cn>.

Sanger, David E. "Senate Agrees to Dilute 'Buy America' Provisions". *New York Times*, 4 February 2009. <http://www.nytimes.com>.

"Vice Minister Yi Xiaozhun of the Ministry of Commerce: China's Overall Economy Achieved Stable Development" (商务部副部长易小准: 商务运行整体平稳), 6 December 2008. <http://finance.sina.com.cn>.

World Trade Organization (WTO). "World Trade Developments in 2008". <http://www.wto.org>.

———. "WTO sees 9 per cent Global Trade Decline in 2009 as Recession Strikes". WTO 2009 Press Releases, 23 March 2009. <http://www.wto.org/english/news_e/pres09_e/pr554_e.htm>.

———. "WTO Secretariat Reports Increase in New Anti-dumping Investigations". WTO 2009 Press Releases, 7 May 2009.

5
Hong Kong's Management of the 2008–09 Financial Crisis

Francis T. Lui

Introduction

Just before Lehman Brothers collapsed, one could hardly say that an asset market bubble was about to burst in Hong Kong. Stock prices had already declined by about one third since the last quarter of 2007. Average housing price was 30 per cent lower than the peak in 1997. The real economy had slowed down, but it was not in severe difficulties. There were no obvious reasons for the Hong Kong Government to stimulate or cool down the economy. Had the global financial crisis not occurred, we would expect that the government would have allowed business to continue as usual. Thus, the crisis provides us with a valuable opportunity to learn how it would respond to a crisis caused by external factors.

The Policy Address of the Hong Kong Government, an important annual event summarizing its views and policies, was delivered by Chief Executive Donald Tsang on 15 October 2008, one month after the fall of Lehman Brothers.[1] This allowed enough time for the government to formulate a preliminary interpretation of what the crisis was, and consider its own possible reactions. The Policy Address clearly regarded the crisis as a severe economic shock coming from outside. Although the government found it "impossible to ascertain its adverse impact", it tried to portray an image that appeared to be positive. The Chief Executive announced that he would form a task force "to address the challenges", help the government to turn the crisis "into new business opportunities and enhance (Hong Kong's) competitiveness."[2] But what was the guiding principle behind the government's policy formulations?

The Policy Address reaffirmed that the principle was "Big Market, Small Government". In a press release on 19 September 2006, Donald Tsang defined it as follows:

> This means that we respond to the needs of the market and do our best to support and promote economic development within the limits of a small government. And the Government should not intervene into any sector of the market, which the private sector can sustain on its own.[3]

The phrase "Big Market, Small Government" was introduced by Donald Tsang to replace the much better known slogan, "positive non-interventionism", which was coined by Hong Kong's former financial secretary, Sir Philip Haddon-Cave, in 1980. Although the latter has often been used to represent the generally *laissez-faire* philosophy of the Hong Kong Government, Tsang (2006) correctly points out that the term is ambiguous. That it is also an inadequate description of the reality in Hong Kong policy can be testified by the fact that the government has been intervening massively in such areas as education, housing, and medical care.[4] In fact, the government at different periods had resorted to different labels to describe its policies. Tsang (2006) summarizes these as follows:

> Sir John Bremridge (Financial Secretary from 1981 to 1986) said: "Your Government remains committed to support of the free market economy." Sir Piers Jacobs (1986 to 1991) said: "The economy will normally be most efficient if market forces are relied on and government intervention in the private sector is kept to a minimum." Sir Hamish Macleod (1991 to 1995) said: "Hong Kong's economic philosophy is not difficult to describe. It is a commitment to enterprises, a commitment to low taxation and a commitment to free markets and free trade." He described this commitment as "what might be called consensus capitalism". When I was Financial Secretary (1995 to 2001), I emphasised "maximum support, minimum intervention and fiscal prudence." Antony Leung (2001 to 2003) saw the government's role as "a proactive market enabler". Our current Financial Secretary Henry Tang upholds the principle of "market leads, government facilitates".

All these statements seem to convey the position that the government would rely mainly on market forces to run the economy and that it would intervene only when necessary. As to the question of when intervention is necessary, the answer is left to the government to decide. The public cannot get an unambiguous answer from these statements.

Can we get a clearer answer to the question of when the government would intervene? The current slogan of "Big

Market, Small Government" does not help either. The political rhetoric used in the definition above still leaves a lot of room for governmental discretion, which is also subject to the uncertainties of political pressure. Thus, the ways in which the government formulates policies to deal with the challenges brought on by the crisis can be regarded as a litmus test for the degree of its commitment to the *laissez-faire* philosophy.

In the next section, I shall discuss the movements of some major variables that track the Hong Kong economy. These can shed light on the intensity of the political pressures that the government had to face during the crisis.

Impact of the Financial Crisis

I will now discuss changes in the nominal and real sectors of the Hong Kong economy before and during the crisis. Probably the two most important kinds of assets owned by the people in Hong Kong are stocks and property. Thus, the prices of these assets, as measured by the Hang Seng Index or a housing price index, are arguably the two most relevant variables in the nominal sector we should pay attention to. For the real sector, I shall focus on the real GDP and unemployment rate.

It is difficult to define when the current global crisis started. Mundell (2009) argues that it can be subdivided into three interconnected crises. The first is the subprime mortgage crisis, which "came about as a result of financial innovations, lax Federal Reserve policies and lenient mortgage regulations". It crystallized on 9–10 August 2007, when the European Central Bank and the U.S. Federal

Reserve System issued $300 billion of credit to avert a collapse of the credit system. The second crisis started with the bankruptcy of Lehman Brothers, which, in Mundell's opinion, was caused by the 25 per cent fall of the U.S. dollar against gold and the euro in the third quarter of 2008. The third crisis, characterized by the contraction of the real economy, and also caused by the strong dollar, occurred at the same time as the second one.

Taking Mundell's interpretation, we can see that the $300 billion injection was able to postpone, but not resolve, a drastic decline in the stock market due to the subprime mortgage crisis. Figure 5.1 shows the movement of the Hang Seng Index from January 2007 to October 2009. If we use the Hang Seng Index as a measure of the impact of the crisis, we can see that after the injection of funds, the index was able to increase by 45 per cent from 10 August 2007 to 30 October 2007. From the October peak to 12 September 2008, the weekend before the Lehman collapse, the Hang Seng Index declined by 38.8 per cent, completely giving up the gain in 2007. During that period, news about the subprime crisis had long been plaguing the financial sector. When the Lehman bankruptcy took place, it was not a bursting of a bubble. Rather, the 43.1 per cent steep decline from 12 September to its bottom level on 27 October 2008 should be interpreted as a panicky reaction on the part of the market to the uncertainties caused by an event that people did not fully understand. It was a period of flight to quality safe assets away from risky securities. The surprising thing is that the adjustment was so fast. It took only one-and-a-half months for the market to bottom out. Exactly one year after it hit the bottom on 27 October 2008, the Hang Seng Index increased by 101 per cent.

Another important variable in the nominal sector is housing price. This can be conveniently tracked by an index compiled by the real estate agency Centaline. Figure 5.2 plots the weekly housing price index against time from the beginning of 2007 to the end of October 2009. The movement of the housing price index follows a similar pattern to that of the Hang Seng Index. Housing price rose throughout 2007 and peaked on 7 March 2008. The latter happened several months after the Hang Seng Index did. It then stagnated and declined moderately until the Lehman bankruptcy. After this it dropped by 17.1 per cent within a short period of three months, until it hit the bottom on 14 December 2008. However, from this bottom, the housing price index reversed its trend. By 25 October 2009, it had gone up by 29.4 per cent. By the fourth quarter of 2009, a popular view in the city is that apartments, especially the luxurious ones, have become so expensive that a bubble may be emerging.

We can therefore see that the effects of the financial crisis on both the stock and housing markets in Hong Kong are deep and serious, but they did not last long. The reversal was fast and powerful. On 20 July 2009, in less than ten and a half months, the Hang Seng Index was able to get back to the pre-Lehman level. The housing market recovery was even faster. On 28 June 2009, the housing price index had already surpassed the 14 September 2008 level again. Was the fast recovery due to the external environment, or was it due to the policy success of the Hong Kong Government?

FIGURE 5.1
Hang Seng Index, 2007–09

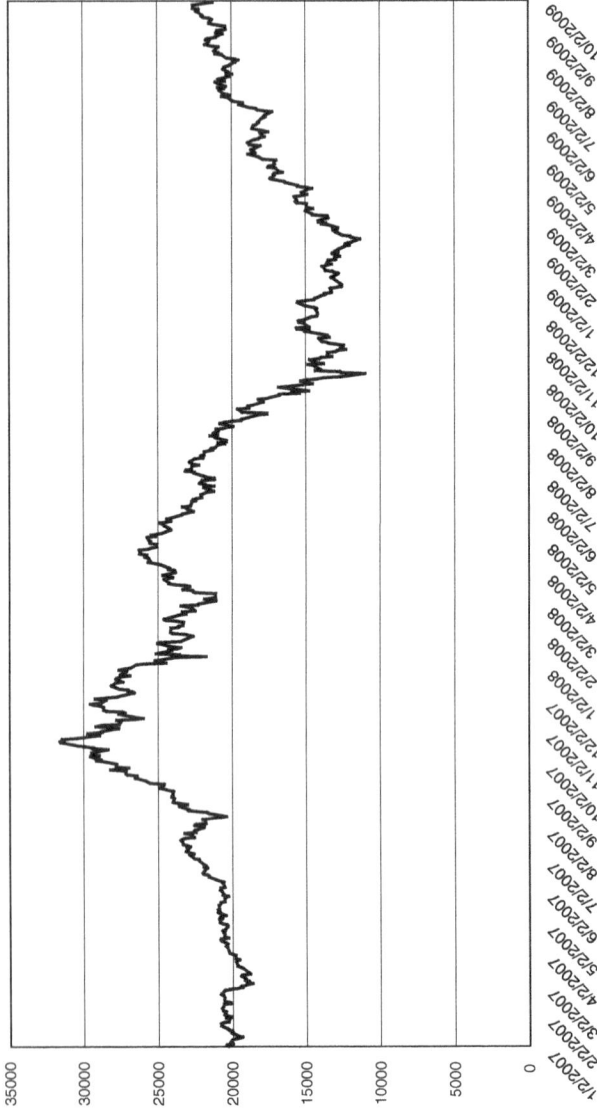

Source: Hong Kong Stock Exchange, <http://www.hkex.com.hk/eng/index.htm>.

FIGURE 5.2
Centaline Housing Price, 2007–09
(10/1997 = 100)

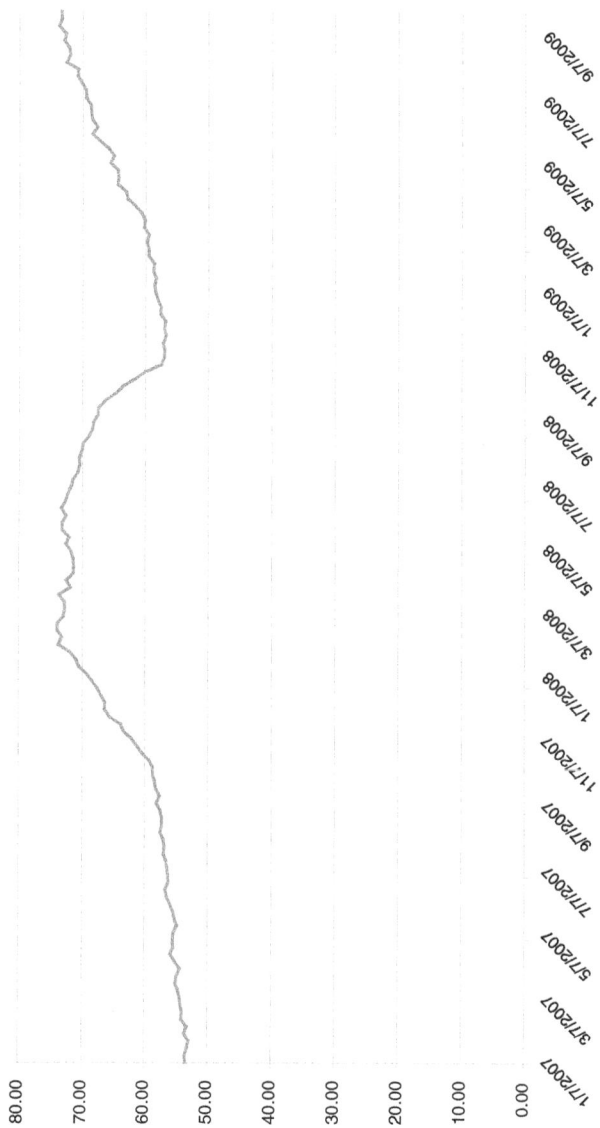

Source: Centadata, <http://www.centadata.com/cci/cci.htm>.

We will now consider the impact of the financial crisis on the real sector. The most relevant variable in this regard is the real GDP. Since seasonal fluctuations of Hong Kong's real GDP are very significant, we have to make the appropriate adjustments in order to get a clearer picture of what has happened. Table 5.1 presents both the quarter-to-quarter seasonally adjusted growth rates and the year-to-year growth rates. Several observations can be made. First, the impact of the financial crisis is substantial. From the first quarter of 2008 to the first quarter of 2009, real GDP growth was –7.8 per cent. A decline of this magnitude is comparable to, but slightly smaller than that of the Asian Financial Crisis, when the annualized quarterly real GDP

TABLE 5.1
Hong Kong's Real GDP Growth Rates, 2007–09

Quarter	Quarter-to-Quarter Seasonally Adjusted Growth	Year-to-Year Growth Rate
2007 Q1	1.1	5.6
2007 Q2	1.7	6.1
2007 Q3	2.0	6.8
2007 Q4	2.1	6.9
2008 Q1	1.0	7.3
2008 Q2	–1.0	4.1
2008 Q3	–0.8	1.5
2008 Q4	–1.9	–2.6
2009 Q1	–4.3	–7.8
2009 Q2	3.3	–3.8
2009 Q3	0.4	–2.4

growth rate once hit −8.1 per cent. Second, seasonally adjusted GDP had already declined for a quarter before the Lehman bankruptcy. Third, the recovery had also been fast. Quarterly real GDP went up by a robust 3.3 per cent in the second quarter of 2009 relative to the first quarter, and continued to rise by another 0.4 per cent in the subsequent quarter. Various macroeconomic forecasts indicate that for the year 2009 as a whole, the decline in real GDP may be in the neighbourhood of 3.3 per cent, which is much smaller than the 6 per cent negative growth in 1998.

Unemployment rate is a variable that can possibly attract even more attention from the government and politicians. Unemployed people are among the biggest losers of a recession. Even if the decline in GDP were not deep, those who had lost their jobs would still have to face a lot of hardships. For much of 2008, unemployment rate in Hong Kong remained at the low level of 3.3 per cent, but the quantitative effect of the Lehman Brothers incident was significant. It had pushed the unemployment rate upwards by 2 percentage points. Although it is too early to tell when the unemployment rate will settle down, the slight decline beginning in the third quarter of 2009 may signal that it had already peaked in the summer. See Figure 5.3.

The situation in the real sector of the economy, as measured by the real GDP and unemployment rate, is consistent with that in the nominal sector. The global financial crisis was able to depress the GDP quickly at a magnitude comparable to that in the Asian Financial Crisis. However, strong recovery also occurred early. The two percentage point rise in unemployment caused hardships, but the effect would be weaker than the 8.7 per cent

FIGURE 5.3
Seasonally Adjusted Unemployment Rate, 2006–09

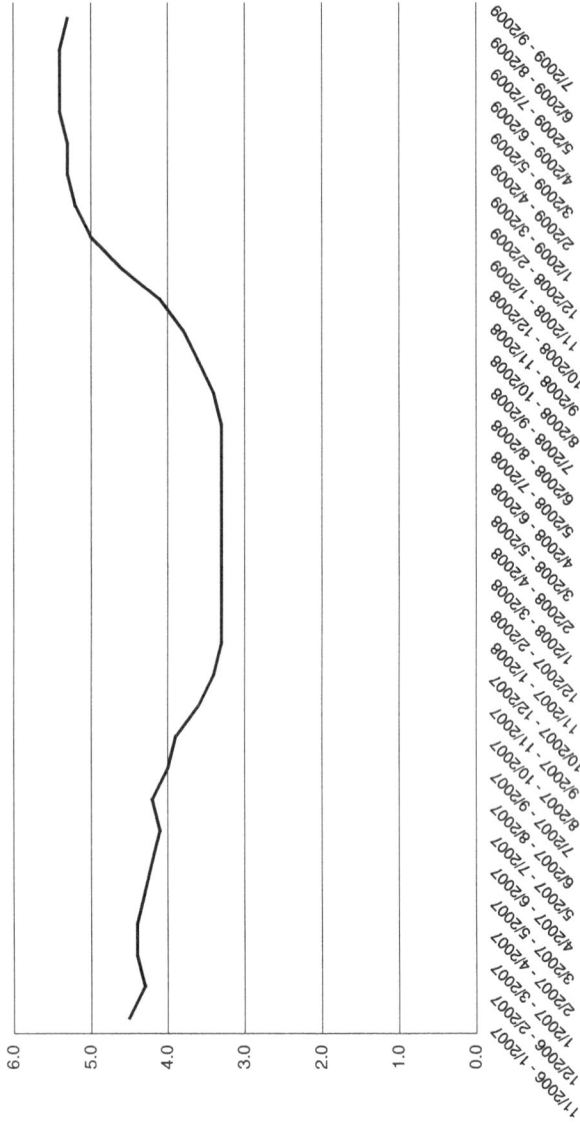

Source: Census and Statistics Department, Hong Kong SAR government.

unemployment rate in the summer of 2003, when the economy had just been inflicted by SARS (Severe Acute Respiratory Syndrome). These phenomena indicate that a great depression, as was widely feared by people all over the world — in governments, media, and business — during the early phase of the crisis, did not materialize. In the near future, it is also unlikely that it will occur. How much credit can the Hong Kong Government claim for a rebound that is almost V-shaped?

Policy Responses

Two major types of strategies are usually considered when governments try to counter the financial crisis. They are those aimed at maintaining stability of financial and banking institutions and those used to stimulate aggregate demand of the economy. This distinction between the two is imperfect because some policies, such as monetary policy, may be intended for both purposes.

Stabilizing Financial and Banking Institutions

Facing the possible threat of a depression, many governments in the world have learned from Friedman and Schwartz (1963) that central banks should play the role of the lender of last resort and that contraction of money supply must be avoided. Even though today's financial and banking system is more complex than that during the time of the Great Depression in the 1930s, some basic principles of maintaining stability still remain valid. If people were fearful that their assets could drastically decline in value, they would resort to selling high-risk securities and holding safer assets. When a central bank injects money into banks or other corporations by buying some of the securities they hold, their portfolios become less susceptible to external shocks. This in turn will increase the willingness of banks to extend loans in the credit market. However, it may take time for this to happen. Money will flow out of the bank's vaults only gradually.

The monetary system of Hong Kong is that of a currency board. As such, there is no central bank, and a monetary policy in the usual sense cannot be pursued. The money supply is not determined by the Hong Kong Monetary Authority. It depends passively on how much foreign currency flows into or out of Hong Kong. In the absence of an operational instrument to control the money supply, an expansionary monetary policy, which has been a key policy for countering the financial crisis in other economies, is not a viable option for Hong Kong.

Even though the Hong Kong Government cannot increase the money supply at its will, except on a very small scale, it does not mean that this had remained a constant during the financial crisis. Figure 5.4 plots M3 against time. The steep rise in M3 (money supply) after August 2007, due to hot money flowing into Hong Kong, coincided with the $300 billion injection of credit by the European Central Bank and the U.S. Fed. After hot money stopped flowing in, M3 declined and remained stagnant for several months in 2008. From August 2007 to August 2008, M3 only increased by 0.16 per cent. Several months after the Lehman collapse, the policy of monetary easing in many countries gradually succeeded in making banks less risk-averse than they had

FIGURE 5.4
M3 in Hong Kong (HK$ plus Foreign Deposits), 2007–09
(HK$ in millions)

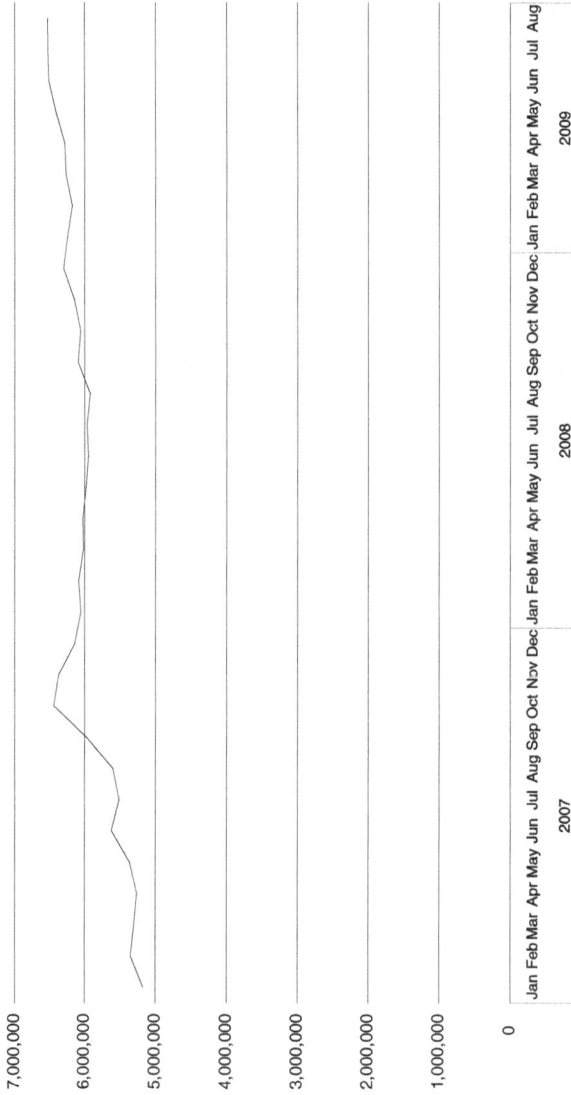

Source: Hong Kong Monetary Authority, <http://www.info.gov.hk/hkma/eng/statistics/index.htm>.

been. Hot money again flowed into Hong Kong. From August 2008 to August 2009, M3 rose by 10.3 per cent. Thus, the same effects of an expansionary monetary policy took place in Hong Kong, even though the government played very little role in this.

In the midst of the uncertainties following the Lehman Brothers collapse — probably due to the downgrading of its credit rating by Moody — there was a run on the Bank of East Asia on 24 September 2008. Although the bank run was quickly ended by the injection of funds by the Hong Kong Monetary Authority and the purchase of shares by the richest man in Hong Kong, it prompted the government to consider new measures to avoid the same thing happening again.

The most important new measure was a change in the Deposit Protection Scheme. Previously, there was a scheme that protected up to HK$100,000 of deposits in an account. On 14 October 2008, the government decided to use the Exchange Fund to guarantee repayment of "all" customer deposits held with all authorized institutions in Hong Kong. The guarantee was to take effect immediately and would last until the end of 2010. The reason that the full protection scheme would last for only two years is to mitigate any moral hazard behaviour on the part of banks. Certain types of deposits, such as time deposits with maturity periods longer than five years, structured deposits, or offshore deposits, were not covered.[5] Although total M3 in Hong Kong exceeds HK$6.5 trillion, the guarantee is generally regarded as credible because the value of the total assets of the Monetary Authority is also very large. It amounted to more than HK$1.8 trillion in August 2009 (HKMA 2009).

Other measures were also introduced in September 2008 to enable the Hong Kong Monetary Authority to become a more effective lender of last resort for troubled banks. These included the provision of liquidity assistance to the banking system and the establishment of a Contingent Bank Capital Facility (Tsang [2009, section 24]). However, there is no evidence showing that these measures played any major role in navigating the economy out of the crisis.

Another incident that had prompted regulatory bodies of the government to take action was the Lehman mini-bonds debacle. These "mini-bonds" were in fact complex structured financial products that were sold by retail banks, which often portrayed them as simple and low-risk products. After Lehman had declared bankruptcy, the value of these "mini-bonds" was in great doubt. Thousands of ordinary investors had lost their lifelong savings.

There were two major problems the government had to resolve. First, buyers of the "mini-bonds" demanded that they should get their money back. This soon became a major political and social event. After months of negotiation, the Securities and Futures Commission (SFC), the Hong Kong Monetary Authority (HKMA), and sixteen distributing banks jointly announced that they had reached an agreement. Its main point was that the banks would offer to repurchase from eligible customers all outstanding mini-bonds at a price equal to 60 per cent of the nominal value of the original investment for customers below the age of sixty-five, and at 70 per cent of the nominal value for customers aged sixty-five and above.[6] Although the majority of customers have accepted the offer, some have refused to do so. It is unclear whether the problem will ever be fully resolved.

The second problem is that there were several regulators whose authority was not clearly delineated. For a long time, there was substantial confusion on whether the HKMA or the SFC was responsible for the lax regulation. On 25 September 2009, the SFC launched a consultation on proposed rule changes related to each stage of the investment life cycle, including pre-sale documentation, disclosure at the point of sale and after, selling practices, and post-sale cooling-off period. On 30 October, the SFC started another consultation on proposals to align the two regulatory regimes under the Companies Ordinance and the Securities and Futures Ordinance for public offers of unlisted structured products. Since the process is still at the public consultation stage, the final outcome is not known yet. Nevertheless, it is fair to say that the crisis has induced the government to re-examine various aspects of the regulatory system.

Stimulating Aggregate Demand

Putting forward a fiscal stimulus package is an important policy component that many governments have used. In the case of Hong Kong, there are other considerations. First, the Basic Law, which is the mini-constitution of Hong Kong, requires that the budget of the government be generally balanced. The fiscal structure is such that it is difficult to increase revenue for the government substantially. Thus, raising expenditure can easily create budget deficits, and therefore violate the Basic Law. Second, Hong Kong operates a currency board, which requires the monetary base be 100 per cent backed up by foreign reserves. In addition, to deter possible monetary attacks, even more foreign reserves would be needed. Any extensive usage of the fiscal reserves, which are managed by the HKMA, would mean a reduction in the ammunition to defend the Hong Kong dollar during an attack. The government and the public therefore tend to be rather conservative in spending matters. Third, previous experience has shown that fiscal reserves of the government could be depleted quickly. In December 1998, fiscal reserves amounted to HK$424.6 billion. The value dropped to HK$252.3 billion by December 2003. Although at the end of 2008, it had increased to HK$531.4 billion, it quickly declined to HK$484.8 billion by June 2009. Large expenditures are not sustainable.

The official response to the financial crisis, as stated in the 2008–09 Policy Address (Tsang [2008]), was measured. Economic discussion focused on long-term policies, such as the integration with China. The major new proposal in this was to set up a task force, later known as the Task Force on Economic Challenges (TFEC), to explore what else could be done.

A series of measures to combat the financial crisis was announced at various points of time, notably after meetings of the TFEC, at the Budget Speech of the financial secretary, or during the Policy Address of the Chief Executive. Here, we will not attempt to be exhaustive. Instead, only the major policies will be discussed.

After the second meeting of the TFEC, which took place on 8 December 2008, the government announced that it would substantially expand the Special Loan Guarantee (Hong Kong Economic and Trade Office 2008). Previously, the government had already established a scheme called the SME Loan Guarantee Scheme that was aimed at helping small and medium sized enterprises get credit in the market. In November that year, the government decided to allow greater flexibility for the system. The new initiative introduced in the December meeting was that the government would increase the maximum commitment to HK$100 billion while continuing to provide 70 per cent loan guarantees. The loan ceiling of each company was raised from HK$1 million to HK$6 million, with HK$3 million being revolving credit. It also allowed all firms except listed companies to apply for the scheme.

The objective of the initiative was obviously to mitigate the credit crunch problem that had plagued many economies. The large amount of money committed, HK$100 billion, was very unusual. It was equal to over one third of Hong Kong's annual government budget. However, this was only a credit guarantee, which might not require actual spending. In fact, the scheme was not as popular as one might believe. The financial secretary reported in his Budget Speech that as of March 2009, there were 3,000 successful applications, involving guarantee for loans of only HK$6 billion.[7] The scheme's contribution to the recovery — which had already been significant in the second quarter of 2009 — would have been very limited.

The TFEC meeting in December also made a number of proposals to create jobs. As in other economies, infrastructure projects were conveniently chosen as a method to increase employment. But most of these projects were not new. It usually takes several years after the government commits to a project before work on it actually starts. The TFEC proposal did nothing except expedite the implementation of old plans. The government claimed that 60,000 jobs, including temporary positions, would be created. It is likely that this is an overestimate since there may be substantial double counting and crowding-out effects that are typically ignored.

A well-known weakness of using infrastructure as a means to stimulate the economy is that in order to expedite the process, the projects are often hastily chosen. Once this happens, these projects may not represent the most efficient use of resources. However, in the case of Hong Kong, this does not seem to be an important issue. The projects had in any case been decided much earlier, the funding had already been earmarked, and a cost-benefit analysis might have been performed. The problem was the slowness in implementation. The urge to create jobs as soon as possible can have the effect of improving the efficiency of the bureaucratic system. However, it would be far-fetched for us to claim that these projects were responsible for leading the economy out of the recession. Most of them had not even started yet when the recovery took place.

Job creation remained a major concern of the government. After the third meeting of the TFEC, more proposals aimed at reducing unemployment were made (Hong Kong Government 2009). These included, among others, requesting statutory bodies to recruit more workers, persuading various organizations to provide more internship opportunities, asking tertiary institutions to hire more tutors and research fellows, and admit more graduate students. These endeavours might have been useful to some extent. However, their effect on the aggregate economy had to be very minor. The government might have put the point of diminishing returns when it tried to identify new options for job creation.

The Budget Speech delivered every year by the Financial Secretary is the occasion for the government to announce how public money is used. In 2009, it was delivered on 25 February, five months after the Lehman collapse. Public expenditure was projected to be 19.4 per cent of GDP, slightly higher than usual. The Financial Secretary believed that he was pursuing a counter-cyclical policy. Whether the Budget of 2009 was counter-cyclical or not has become an issue. In March 2008 when the economy was performing well and the government had a record high budget surplus, there were several aggressive programmes to return wealth to the people. In the contracting year of 2009, there were very few such "candies", which was the nickname used for various forms of subsidies from the government. Some people believed that these proposed expenditures were totally contrary to the idea of a counter-cyclical policy. The government's consolidated deficit would be HK$39.9 billion, or 2.4 per cent of GDP. If we examine the expenditures that are directly targeted for the creation of jobs, we do not see large sums involved, despite the claim that the Budget was counter-cyclical. The total was only HK$1.65 billion, which would have been around 0.5 per cent of the government budget.

Despite the small amount, the money was earmarked for a large number of uses. These included a subsidy for employers to hire middle-aged or disabled people, funding to help those who had lost their jobs during the financial crisis to find new jobs, a subsidy to employers to hire university graduates as interns, funding to repair and maintain dilapidated buildings, a subsidy to help organizers host cultural events, funding to enhance energy efficiency in government buildings, and so on.[8]

In subsequent meetings of the TFEC and also in the 2009 Policy Address delivered in October (Tsang 2009*b*), we saw fewer measures that were supposed to be aimed at rescuing the economy from the financial crisis. Rather, strategies for long-term development were stressed again. Considerable time was devoted to the discussion of the four traditional pillars of the Hong Kong economy, financial services, tourism, trading and logistics, and professional services, and six additional industries in which Hong Kong might have a comparative advantage. The six industries are: education services, medical services, testing and certification services, environmental industries, innovation and technology, and cultural and creative industries. Apparently, the government has taken the opportunity and use the pressures induced by the financial crisis to introduce more diversification in the economy.

Conclusion

Faced with one of the most serious financial crises in modern history, governments would be foolish to do nothing. Politically, this could easily lead to their downfall. However, would proactive counter-cyclical fiscal policy work, or would an expansionary monetary policy be more appropriate?

There are arguments for and against fiscal expansion. For such a policy to work, the multiplier of government expenditure has to be bigger than one. But estimates based on dynamic models generally indicate that it is less than one, which implies that using up one dollar would result in less than one dollar of benefit, a situation that economists generally do not like.

Another argument is that the crisis may have created a liquidity trap, where the interest rate is so low that it cannot be suppressed any more. If such is the case, fiscal policy may be the only instrument to use. It may be true that interest rates for low-risk securities are close to zero. However, it does not mean that cheap loans are accessible to most corporations or consumers who want to borrow funds. Banks would like to impose very high interest rates on their loans to compensate for the risks they have to take. Reducing the "risk premium" would be an important step in stimulating the economy. Expanding the supply of money or the supply of low-risk bonds would improve the portfolios of many banks. When they hold more low-risk securities, they will be more willing to grant loans at lower interest rates.

Since Hong Kong operates under a currency board, there cannot be any full-scale monetary policy. Despite its passivity in providing money supply, the inflow of money, possibly due to the money easing policy in other economies, has contributed to asset inflation and the recovery of the real economy.

From the fall of Lehman to now, the Hong Kong Government has pursued various forms of expansionary fiscal policies. However, either because their scales were very small or because they were generally implemented *after* the recovery had started, it is hard to argue that they were instrumental in rescuing the economy.

The Hong Kong Government itself may not be sure what economic principle it should subscribe to. The debate on whether it should be "positive non-interventionism" or "Big Market, Small Government" may not be meaningful at all. On the other hand, the fact that it has not done much during this crisis could be interpreted from another perspective. *Laissez faire* still works well for the small open economy of Hong Kong. Otherwise, how is it possible that it has walked out of this financial crisis intact?

NOTES

1. See Tsang (2008).
2. See Section 20 of the Policy Address.
3. See Tsang (2006).
4. For a more detailed discussion on "positive non-interventionism", see Cheung (2000) and Cheung (2006).
5. See Bank of China (2008) for more details.
6. See Securities and Futures Commission (2009) for the details of the agreement.
7. See Tsang (2009*a*), Section 24.
8. See Sections 27 and 28 of the 2009 Budget (Tsang 2009*a*).

REFERENCES

Bank of China. "Deposit Protection Questions & Answers — About the Deposit Protection Scheme", 2008. <http://www.bochk.com/images/upload/retail/pdf/QandA1_en.pdf>.

Cheung, Anthony B.L. "New Interventionism in the Making: Interpreting State Interventions in Hong Kong after the Change in Sovereignty". *Journal of Contemporary China* 9, no. 24 (2000): 291–308.

Cheung, Steven N.S. (张五常). "何谓自由经济?" (What is 'Free Economy'?). *East Asia Economic Review* 20 and 22, October 2006. <http://www.e-economic.com/info/8730-1.htm>.

Friedman, Milton and Anna J. Schwartz. *A Monetary History of the United States 1867–1960*. Princeton, New Jersey: Princeton University Press, 1963.

Hong Kong Economic and Trade Office. "Chief Executive Announces Economic Stimulus Package". News Release, Hong Kong SAR Government, 8 December 2008. <http://www.hketousa.gov.hk/usa/press/2008/dec08/120808_1.htm>.

Hong Kong Monetary Authority (HKMA). *Monthly Statistical Bulletin*, October 2009. <http://www.info.gov.hk/hkma/eng/statistics/msb/index.htm>.

Hong Kong Government. "CE Announces New Measures to Tackle Financial Tsunami". Press Release, 22 January 2009.

Mundell, Robert. "The Cause of the Crisis and Its Implications for China and the International Exchange Rate System". Speech delivered at the 2nd Forum on Future Development of China, Nansha, Guangdong Province, 30 October 2009.

New York Times. "Run on Bank of East Asia Prompts $500m Hong Kong Cash Injection", 25 September 2008.

Securities and Futures Commission. "SFC, HKMA and 16 Banks Reach Agreement on Minibonds". Press Release, 22 July 2009. <http://www.sfc.hk/sfcPressRelease/EN/sfcOpen DocServlet?docno=09PR100>.

Tsang, John. "The 2009–10 Budget". Speech by the financial secretary, Hong Kong SAR Government, 25 February 2009*a*.

Tsang, Donald. " 'Big Market, Small Government' Key". Press Release, Hong Kong SAR Government, 19 September 2006. <http://news.gov.hk/en/category/ontherecord/060919/html/060919en11001.htm>.

———. "The 2008–09 Policy Address: Embracing New Challenges". Hong Kong SAR Government, 2008. <http://www.policyaddress.gov.hk/08-09/eng/docs/policy.pdf>.

———. "The 2009–10 Policy Address: Breaking New Ground Together". Hong Kong SAR Government, 2009*b*. <http://www.policyaddress.gov.hk/09-10/eng/docs/policy.pdf>.

6
Taiwan's Policy Responses to the Financial Tsunami in 2008

Shen Chung-Hua

Introduction

Since August 2007, the U.S subprime mortgage crisis has not only threatened the U.S. economy into a recession, but affected the global financial system. The spread of the U.S. financial storm triggered a global credit crunch and tipped Western economies into recession. World GDP growth decrease from −1.7 per cent in 2007 to −2.9 per cent in 2008 (World Bank 2008). Many countries responded by launching massive public investment programmes and employing expansionary fiscal policies to weather this once-in-a-century financial tsunami. In the United States besides the well publicized US$100 billion approved by Congress, the Federal Reserve attempted to bail out institutions and markets with about $1.3 trillion in investments in various risky products. In addition, many developed and developing countries also provided astronomical amounts to rescue the economy.

This chapter reports on how the Taiwanese Government rescued its economy during the financial crisis, with particular focus on small and medium enterprises (SME). During the financial crisis, Taiwan's economy also dipped to the bottom. While its GDP growth was recorded as 4.2 per cent, 4.8 per cent, 5.7 per cent, and 1.9 per cent from 2005 to 2008, the expected GDP growth rate in 2009 was –4.0, a record low in history since 1980. To safeguard the stability of Taiwan's economic growth by stimulating domestic demand as a means of sustaining the economic growth momentum, the government adopted the short- and long-term policies to revitalize the economy. With respect to the short-term policies, the government issued consumption vouchers for an immediate stimulus measure in January 2009. It also announced the "three-pillar support policy" to restore the confidence of the Taiwanese people. This "three-pillar support" means that the government would support banks, bank would support enterprises, and enterprises would support their workers. For its long-term policies, the government adopted a four-year project (2009–12) to expand and accelerate the implementation of public works, with the aim of creating a second wave of economic revitalization effect to augment the benefits generated by the consumption voucher scheme.

For the "three-pillars support policy", the core part of the first pillar was realized through the unlimited deposit insurance announced in September 2008 to avoid any bank runs. The core part of the second pillar is to provide a high guarantee coverage ratio when SMEs borrow money from banks. The third pillar depends on enterprises weathering the financial crisis and keeping their employees. Our focus is on the second pillar.

Typically, SMEs are small in size, weak in financial resources, and unsound in their accounting systems. They are especially short of tangible assets which more than often are required to serve as collateral when applying for external finance. Moreover, the information asymmetry between SMEs and banks is substantial since SMEs data might be sparse and not particularly reliable because their financial statements are generally not audited. A recent study has shown that SMEs not only report higher financing obstacles than large firms, but the effect of these financing constraints is stronger for SMEs than for large firms (Beck, Demirgüç-Kunt and Maksimovic 2004). Both high transaction costs related to relationship lending and the high risk intrinsic to SME lending explain the reluctance of finance institutions to reach out to SME (Beck et al. 2008). All these factors have made SMEs marginal clients to financial institutions.

Because of the serious information asymmetry in SMEs, it is often difficult for banks to conduct successful risk evaluations. The result is that banks are reluctant to lend money to SMEs. To remedy this situation, the Taiwanese Government has consistently provided financial and other assistance to SMEs. The bureau of Small and Medium Enterprise Guarantee Fund (SMEG) is designed to minimize the gap in this information asymmetry. During the crisis, the ratio of guaranteed coverage was raised by SMEG. On the surface, one could argue that the policy is futile since SMEs lending still decreased even though coverage ratios were raised. However, lending to SMEs may in fact have increased, relative to the equilibrium level of loans during the crisis. If the guaranteed coverage ratios have not been raised, lending might even dropped. In academic jargon, the evaluation should be compared with "equilibrium" loans and not simple observed rates (see Shen 2002 for the meaning of "equilibrium loan").

No doubt, raising the guarantee coverage ratio to close to 100 per cent created a moral hazard problem. That is the reason a partial credit guarantee system was adopted. Assisting SMEs requires the government to have strong fiscal reserves to provide the necessary financial support. However, because of the systemic risk rising, the government could not but inject huge funds to rescue the severely hit economy. Many developed countries, such as the United States, the United Kingdom, and many European countries also adopted similar policies. It can be likened to rescuing the sick in intensive care by applying an electric shock to them, without being too concerned about how the shock would affect their health in the future.

Past Economic Performance

Table 6.1 reports Taiwan's past economic outlook from 1997 to 2008. The average GDP growth rate during the period 1997–2000 was 5.7 per cent and it dropped slightly over the years after that. The GDP growth rate was merely 1.9 per cent in 2008. The decrease in GDP growth was due to a decrease in domestic demand whose share of GDP fell from 5.3 per cent in the period 1997–2000 to –0.8 per cent in 2008. By contrast, the net external demand increased from 0.36 per cent to 2.67 per cent in the same periods.

Our focus is on private investment. In 2008, private fixed investment's contribution to GDP growth was –1.15

TABLE 6.1
Sources of Taiwan's Economic Growth, 1997–2008

Unit contribution in percentage points

Year	GDP growth rate (%)	Domestic demand	Private consumption	Private fixed investment	Public expenditure	Government fixed investment	Net external demand	Exports of goods and services
1997–2000 (averaged)	5.67	5.30	3.54	1.72	0.31	-0.01	0.36	4.90
2001–2007 (averaged)	3.83	1.63	1.38	0.30	-0.19	-0.23	2.19	4.56
2005	4.16	1.53	1.76	0.05	0.33	-0.06	2.63	4.66
2006	4.80	1.34	1.02	0.54	-0.42	-0.23	3.46	6.48
2007	5.70	1.90	1.31	0.49	-0.01	-0.14	3.81	5.86
2008	1.87	-0.80	-0.16	-1.15	0.22	0.04	2.67	2.47

Source: The Directorate-General of Budget, Accounting and Statistics (DGBAS), Executive Yuan.

per cent, a fall larger than that registered by domestic demand on private consumption.

Bank Loans

We can also investigate the domestic demand for bank lending. Figure 6.1 indicates how the total loans to the four sectors — public enterprise, private enterprise, individuals, and government — fell at the beginning of 2009. Thus, demand was much weaker in 2009.

We first classify Taiwan's banks into four groups based on their ownership, namely, quasi-government banks (hereafter, quasi-public bank), private banks, foreign bank branches (foreign branches), and foreign bank subsidiaries. The quasi-government banks refer to banks whose controlling shareholder is the government. Typically, the percentage of shares owned by the governments exceed 25 per cent through direct and indirect shareholdings. Controlling shareholders are in the private sector for private banks. In general, foreign bank subsidiaries are registered in their host country, but their controlling shareholders are foreigners. In our case, foreign bank subsidiaries refer to those foreign banks that have purchased Taiwanese local distressed banks since 2006. Thus the loan amounts of foreign bank subsidiaries are available from then. Foreign bank branches are self-explanatory. See Appendix A for a detailed description of these four types of banks.

We will discuss three types of loans next, that is, loans to public enterprise, private and SME, provided by the above four groups of banks. In Figure 6.2, the four graphs show the loans to public enterprises by the four different

FIGURE 6.1
Loan Amounts to the Four Different Sectors, 2004–08

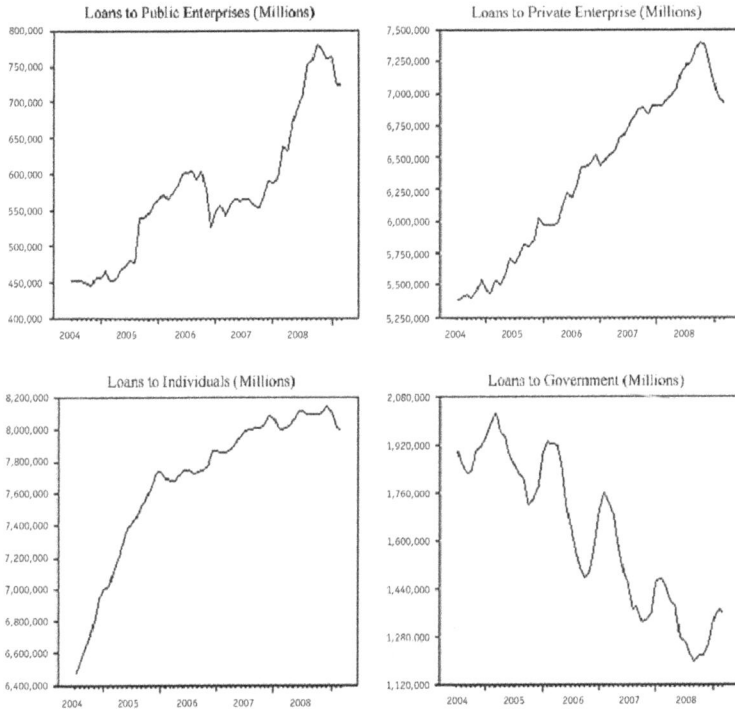

Sources: TEJ (Taiwan Economic Journal Co. Ltd.); Directorate-General of Budget, Accounting and Statistics, Executive Yuan, R.O.C. (Taiwan); and Financial Supervisory Commission, Executive Yuan, R.O.C. (Taiwan).

types of banks, respectively. In each panel, we plot the amount of loans (solid line) against the loan growth rate (dotted line). The amount of loans increased over the years, but started to drop in July 2008 for quasi-public banks. The amount of loans rose in 2006, but started to fluctuate in 2007 for private banks. The number decreased over the years from 2006 for foreign bank subsidiaries, and dropped

FIGURE 6.2
Loans to Public Enterprises by Four Types of Banks, 1998–2009

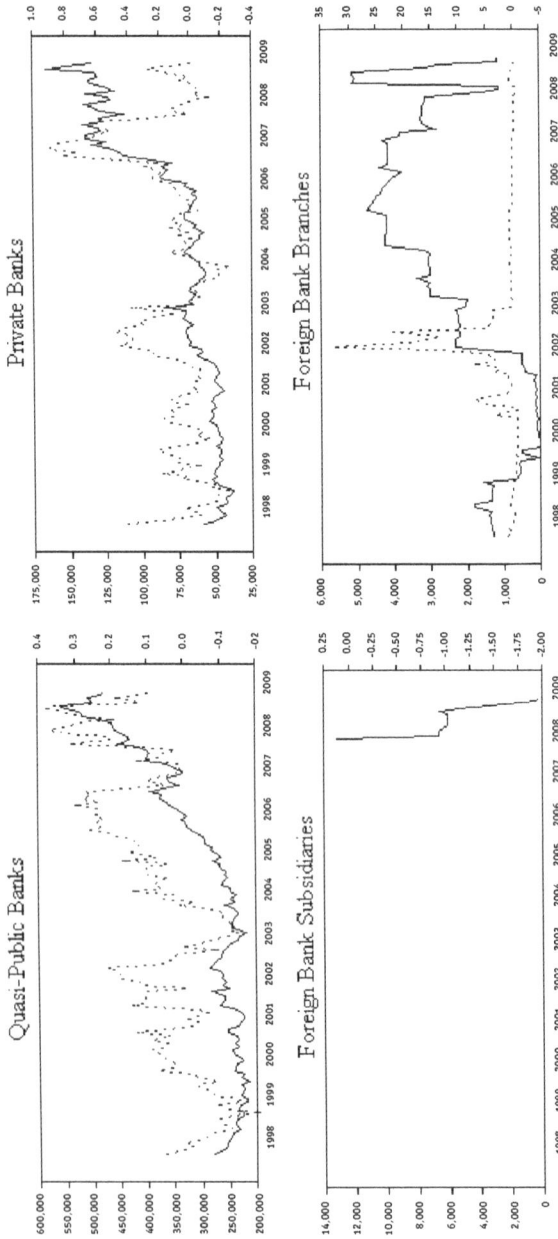

Notes: 1. Loan amounts = Solid line (left scale)
       2. Loan growth = dotted line (right scale)

Sources: TEJ (Taiwan Economic Journal Co. Ltd.); Directorate-General of Budget, Accounting and Statistics, Executive Yuan, R.O.C. (Taiwan); and Financial Supervisory Commission, Executive Yuan, R.O.C. (Taiwan).

substantially at the beginning of 2009 for foreign bank branches. Thus, while quasi-public banks increased their loans before the financial tsunami, foreign sectors trimmed their loan. This may be due to the decrease on both the demand and supply side. Moreover, public enterprises continued to borrow from private banks, though the borrowing momentum was weak.

Figure 6.3 shows loans to the private sector. Typically, loans to the private sector by quasi-public banks and private banks fell during the financial tsunami. For both types of foreign banks, however, the amount of loans decreased earlier than the first two types of banks in 2006–07 and plunged during the financial tsunami. Foreign banks have either been cherry-picking or projecting a pessimistic view of business growth in Taiwan since 2006.

Figure 6.4 depicts loans to SMEs. The amount of loans decreased in 2008 and their growth rate deceased much earlier than that. Here too, the growth rate of foreign banks declined even faster, followed by that of private banks and quasi-public banks. We will discuss in detail the loans to SME in the next subsection.

One of the big falls in private investment is the decrease in the number of the small and medium enterprises during the financial tsunami. If we divide SMEs into manufacturing and services SMEs, the lion share of the former and some of the latter have moved to China. This subsection discusses the role of SMEs.

Table 6.2 reports the contribution of SMEs to the economy from 2005–07. In 2007, there were approximately 1,237,000 million SMEs in Taiwan, which accounted for 97.6 per cent of all enterprises. Likewise, in terms of

FIGURE 6.3
Loans to Private Enterprises by Four Types of Banks, 1998–2009

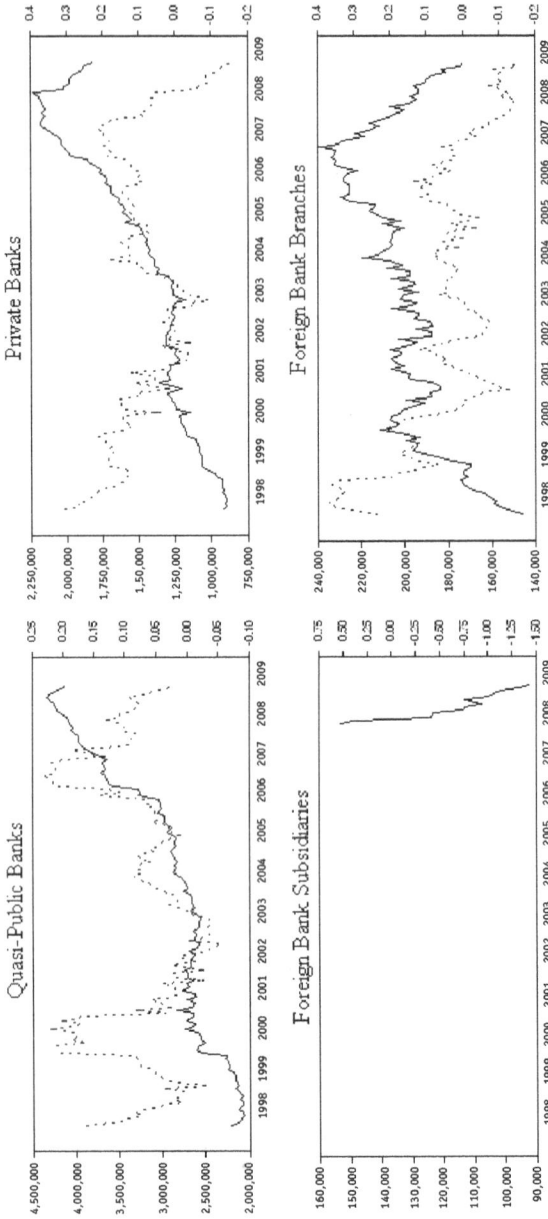

Notes: 1. Loan amounts = Solid line (left scale)
          2. Loan growth = dotted line (right scale)
Sources: TEJ (Taiwan Economic Journal Co. Ltd.); Directorate-General of Budget, Accounting and Statistics,
Executive Yuan, R.O.C. (Taiwan); and Financial Supervisory Commission, Executive Yuan, R.O.C. (Taiwan).

FIGURE 6.4
Loans to SMEs by Four Types of Banks, 1996–2009

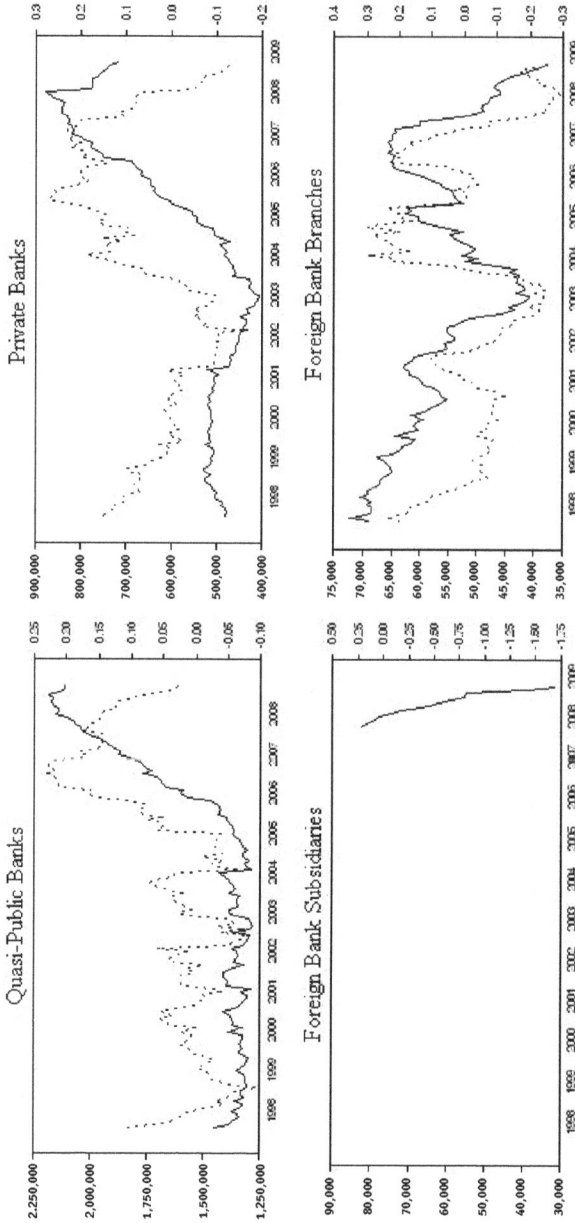

Quasi-Public Banks

Private Banks

Foreign Bank Subsidiaries

Foreign Bank Branches

Notes: 1. Loan amounts = Solid line (left scale)
2. Loan growth = dotted line (right scale)
Sources: TEJ (Taiwan Economic Journal Co. Ltd.); Directorate-General of Budget, Accounting and Statistics, Executive Yuan, R.O.C. (Taiwan); and Financial Supervisory Commission, Executive Yuan, R.O.C. (Taiwan).

TABLE 6.2
Basic Statistics of SMEs in Taiwan, 2005–07

Indicator	2005	2006	2007
SMEs/All enterprises (%)			
Percentage of SMEs/total enterprises	97.8	97.77	97.63
Percentage of total employment			
sustained by SMEs	76.93	76.66	77.12
Sales value	29.46	29.84	28.34
Direct export	17.60	17.89	17.02
Credit to SMEs/Credit to all			
enterprises (%)	16.06	17.16	18.21

Source: Handbook of Taiwan SME Policy Report.

employment, SMEs provided 7,939,000 jobs, which kept 77.1 per cent of the workforce employed. The highest concentration of SMEs can be seen in three industries, wholesale and retail (672,794), manufacturing (136,887) and accommodation and food and drinks establishments (107,464). While the contribution of SMEs to the economy was large, the lending to SMEs out of the total lending was only around 15 per cent.

Panels A and B in Table 6.3 examine whether lending decreased during the Asian Financial Crisis of 1998–99 and the financial tsunami of 2008–09 respectively. Panel A shows that the only decreases in lending were loans to public enterprises by quasi-government banks during the Asian Financial Crisis. In fact, the lending to other sectors by other banks increased even during the crisis. On the whole, loans still increased during the Asian Crisis to some extent.

TABLE 6.3
Bank Lending Decreases During the Two Crises

Asian Financial Crisis 1998–99

Panel A	Loan to Public Enterprises	Loan to Private Enterprise	Loans to SME
Quasi State-Owned Banks	yes	X	X
Private Banks	X	X	X
Foreign Banks	X	X	X
Private Banks controlled by foreigners	X	X	X

Financial Tsunami 2008–09

Panel B	Loan to Public Enterprises	Loan to Private Enterprise	Loans to SME
Quasi-State-Owned Bank	X	X	X
Private Banks	X	Yes	Yes
Foreign Bank Subsidiaries	—	Yes	Yes
Foreign Bank branches	—	Yes	Yes

Notes: 1. Yes = the lending decreased
2. X = the lending did not decrease

Panel B examines lending during the financial tsunami of 2008–09. Quasi-government banks were the only type of banks that increased their lending during this period. In contrast, private banks, foreign bank subsidiaries and foreign bank branches cut their lending to the private sector and SMEs. This shows that foreign banks and private banks were reluctant to lend money to SMEs, making the decrease in lending to them more pronounced than that to other sectors. What it means is that SMEs were easily financially constrained during the crisis.

Future Economic Outlook

We now investigate which sector of the GDP caused the drop in Taiwan's economic growth rate in 2009. The 2009 GDP growth rate has not yet been officially published, and the figures for 2009 are based on the projection of relevant government offices.

To analyse the factors contributing the GDP growth rate, we can rewrite the GDP definition as:

$$\text{GDP} = w_c\, C + w_{Ip}\, I_P + w_g\, G + w_{Ig}\, I_G + w_{x-m}\, (X - M)$$
$$= \text{GDP\_C} + \text{GDP\_Ip} + \text{GDP\_G} + \text{GDP\_Ig} + \text{GDP\_x–m}$$

where GDP, C, I_P, G, I_G, and $(X - M)$ denote the growth rates of gross domestic product, consumption, private investment, government consumption, public investment, and net export, respectively; weights w_c, w_{Ip} w_g w_{Ig}, and w_{x-m}, are the percentage of the five above components over GDP, respectively and are referred to "five GDP shares". Lastly, variables GDP_C, GDP_Ip, GDP_G, GDP_Ig,

GDP_x–m are the contributions of the above five sectors to the GDP growth rate.

The five GDP shares, w_c, w_{Ip}, w_g w_{Ig} and w_{x-m}, were estimated to be 62, 16, 13, 5, (74–70), respectively in 2008, but they were expected to be 62, 10, 13, 6, (64–56) in 2009. It is evident that share of the private investment fell more than the other sectors.

With respect to the growth rates of these five sectors, the growth rate of private investment was the only sector expected to decrease by more than 1 per cent in 2009. Private investment comprises fixed investment and enterprise inventory investment, which were expected to decrease down to NTD 500 and 76.6 billion respectively, making their expected growth rates to be almost –27 per cent and –14 per cent respectively. Thus, the total drop in private investment would be –41 per cent, which is a record high in history. This sharp fall in investment, together with its 10 per cent share in GDP, make the total contribution of the private investment to GDP growth rate (GDP_Ig) –4.4 per cent. Also, the contribution of remaining four sectors, GDP_c, GDP_G, GDP_IG, GDP_x–m, are 0.12, 0.37, 0.53, –0.66, respectively, making the expected GDP growth in 2009 to be:

$$0.12 - 4.40 + 0.37 + 0.53 + 0.66 = -4.04\%.$$

Because the largest fall would result from the shrinkage in private investment, the government has proposed injecting 500 billion NTD to revitalize the economy over four years, with 149.2 billion NTD given out in 2009. While this sum is much smaller than the private investment fall of 500 billion NTD, it is meant to catalyze the economy and the hope is that the private sector can be revitalized by this policy stimulus.

The decrease in private investment was due to outgoing foreign direct investment to China and demand falls in the local market. The rising share of public investment resulted from the government policy of stimulating public investment. The share of two, private and government, consumption has remained the same in two years. The share of the net export increased, but both export and import shrank.

Policy Responses

The government's "three-pillars policy" to help the country withstand the recent recession was explained at the beginning of this chapter. It refers to the government supporting banks, banks supporting enterprises, and enterprises supporting their workers. The second pillar has been useful as banks would now extend loans for an additional six months from 2009 to enterprises, which have normal operations and constant interest payments. Moreover, Taiwan SMEG should (1) raise its guarantee coverage; (2) launch "Measure of Encouraging Financial Institutions to Actively Extend Loans to SMEs through Credit Guarantee Mechanism"; (3) increase the maximum amount of guaranteed loans for a single enterprise; (4) increase credit line under the Authorized Approach; (5) loosen restrictions on the loan-to-sales ratio; loosen restrictions on the liability ratio.

Because the Taiwan economy was severely hit during the financial crisis, the Taiwan Government proposed the NTD 500-billion "Special Act for Expanding Investment in Public Works" (hereafter the ACT) over the next four years to revitalize the economy. Table 6.4 shows the details of the ACT. The six main targets are (1) completing a fast and convenient transportation network, (2) building a safe and disaster-free environment, (3) raising the quality of the cultural and living environment, (4) strengthening the national competitiveness infrastructure, (5) improving offshore island transport facilities, and fostering prime R&D manpower, and (6) helping to stabilize schooling and employment. The policy contains both short-term and long-run objectives, which it hopes would make economic growth sustainable.

As mentioned above, the proposed NTD-500-billion increase in public investment intended to compensate the drop of NTD 500 billion in private fixed investment. However, this NTD-500-billion public investment is to be spent over four years (2009–12), with NTD 150 billion (30.2 per cent) earmarked for 2009, 160 billion (32.1) for 2010, 105 billion (21 per cent) for 2011, and 84 billion (16.7 per cent) for 2012. Though they are designed to offset the decrease in private fixed investment, they are not all spent immediately in 2009. It is expected that this public investment would play the role of motivating and triggering private investment. Public investment should not crowd out private investment. However, it is known that the multiplier effect of public investment is smaller than that of private investment. Figuring out ways of how to encourage the private sector invest is still an issue.

TABLE 6.4
Project to Expand Investment in Public Works — Six Main Targets, 2009–12

Unit: NT$ billions

Six main targets	Subprojects	2009	2010	2011	2012	Total
(i) Completing a fast and convenient transportation network	18 subprojects, including the Nangang MRT line eastern extension, the Xinyi MRT line, grade separation of railways, railway safety improvement, and widening the Wuyang section of Freeway 1.	24.3426	45.0951	42.5350	26.5636	138.5363 (27.7%)
(ii) Building a safe and disaster-free environment	8 subprojects, including the urgent rebuilding of old bridges on provincial highways, remediation of land subsidence, strengthening of old school buildings, and disaster-prevention slope management.	31.0561	40.6874	15.2111	12.3489	99.3035 (19.9%)

(iii) Raising the quality of the cultural and living environment	20 subprojects, including extending the network of bicycle trails, reducing the piped-water leakage rate, rebuilding retail markets, constructing sewers, and regenerating farm villages.	48.3810	38.7895	20.2046	19.4346	126.8097 (25.4%)
(iv) Strengthening the national competitiveness infrastructure	13 subprojects, including the MRT link to Taoyuan Airport, the national ICT infrastructure, urban renewal related work, and coastal regeneration.	16.9719	27.6.405	25.3524	24.6597	94.6245 (18.9 %)
(v) Improving offshore island transport facilities	3 subprojects for developing offshore island transport facilities.	0.6553	1.2245	0.9930	0.5955	3.4683 (0.7 %)

continued on next page

TABLE 6.4 — *cont'd*

Unit: NT$ billions

Six main targets	Subprojects	2009	2010	2011	2012	Total
(vi) Fostering prime R&D manpower, and helping to stabilize schooling and employment	2 subprojects for creating a schooling safety net and cultivating high-grade manpower to promote employment.	29,2569	7.2318	0.7690	0.000	37.2577 (7.4 %)
Total	64 subprojects	150.6638 (30.2%)	160.6688 (32.1%)	105.0651 (21.0%)	83.6023 (16.7%)	500.00

Details of the Second Pillar:
SME Guarantee Ratios

In order to assist SMEs in seeking external financing, the government established the Small and Medium Enterprise Guarantee Fund (SMEG) in 1974. Its main objective was to provide financial assistance to small and medium enterprises that have been affected by rising inflation and the recession brought on by the oil crisis, and to facilitate their access to finance. National economic and financial policies were aligned with the mission and operation of SMEG.

Table 6.5 shows the continuing paid-in capital to SMEG from donations made by the central government, local governments, contracted financial institutions, and other agencies. Up to the end of 2008, donations received totalled NT$80.58 billion (including separate funds for special guarantee programmes), 79.5 per cent of which were from the central and local governments, 17.9 per cent from the contracted financial institutions, and 2.6 per cent from other agencies. At the end of 2008 its net worth totalled NT$27.96 billion (including separate funds for special guarantee programmes).

When the SME sector itself is in severe recession, SMEG faces the dilemma of whether to raise its guarantee coverage ratio. This is because the current Partial Credit Guarantee (PCG) system, which has been adopted around the world, attempts to provide a balance between moral hazard and systemic risk.

First, if SMEG provides full guarantee coverage, it solves the systemic risk problem, but aggravates the moral hazard problem. Under such circumstances, banks have little incentive to monitor borrowers and therefore subprime or

TABLE 6.5
Paid-in Capital in SMEG, 2005–08

Unit: NT$ millions

Fiscal Year	2005		2006		2007		2008	
	Number	%	Number	%	Number	%	Number	%
Increased Capital	6,306.32	100	7,056.71	100	6,980.54	100	8,560.12	100
Government	5,250.00	83	5,490.00	78	5,000.00	71	6,500.00	75
Financial Institutions	1,056.32	17	1,486.71	21	1,970.54	28	2,057.62	24
Other Agencies, Enterprises	—	—	1.13	1	10.00	1	2.50	1

even non-qualified borrowers can obtain funds. Furthermore, the full guarantee coverage tends to increase the fiscal deficit and may yield considerable non-performing loans, which will become a burden for taxpayers shortly.

On the other hand, if no guarantee is provided, the moral hazard problem is minimized, but systemic risk increases. Under this condition, the strong information asymmetry between banks and SMEs makes banks unwilling to lend. SMEs are financially constrained even if they have sound financial conditions. Unemployment may therefore increase. This information asymmetry becomes even worse during a financial crisis, which may then turn the condition into systemic risk and further increases the unemployment rate. To solve this dilemma, partial credit guaranteed funds have become popular around the world (Beck, Klapper and Mendoza 2008).

Facing the recent once-in-a-century financial crisis, the Taiwan Government decided to tackle systemic risk first by raising the coverage ratio. While Taiwan is not exceptional in adopting this policy (the United States, the United Kingdom, Germany, Japan, Korea, and other developed and developing countries also did this), it created extremely easy monetary and fiscal policies. Asset prices, including stock and house prices, jumped substantially from the start of 2010. The challenge ahead is knowing when to end these lax policies.

There are four approaches the SMEG can use to evaluate a credit application for granting a loan guarantee. They are normal, authorized, and package guarantees, and direct credit guarantee. The first three account for about 99 per cent of all guarantee applications and are all part of what is known as the indirect guarantee approach. The remaining 1 per cent use the direct guarantee approach. The performance of each approach can be represented by its guarantee ratio.

Figure 6.5 shows the movements of the four guarantee ratios. The four ratios have been increasing over the years, from 2007 to the third quarter of 2009 to help SMEs obtain funds. This fulfils the goal of the second pillar: banks supporting enterprises.

Figure 6.6 depicts the trend of loans to SMEs (bold solid line), loan guarantee applications (grey solid line), and loan guarantee approvals (dotted line) by the four types of banks. The first line is set against the right hand axis while the other lines are set against the left hand axis of the graphs. Loan guarantee applications and loan guarantee applications are usually parallel with each other, but not always.

The figure shows that applications for loan guarantees have been decreasing regardless of the type of banks we are looking at, indicating that banks are less willing to lend money to SMEs even when there were guarantees. The situation is even worse with foreign bank subsidiaries and branches, which have withdrawn lending to the SME market. Private banks have also decreased their approvals to them. To resolve the current dilemma in the SME market, full financial support may be just one of the solutions, finding their niche markets successfully may be equally important.

Conclusion

The decrease of GDP growth in Taiwan in 2009 is due mainly to the fall in private investment. Of the enterprises

FIGURE 6.5
Guarantee Coverage Ratio, 2004–09

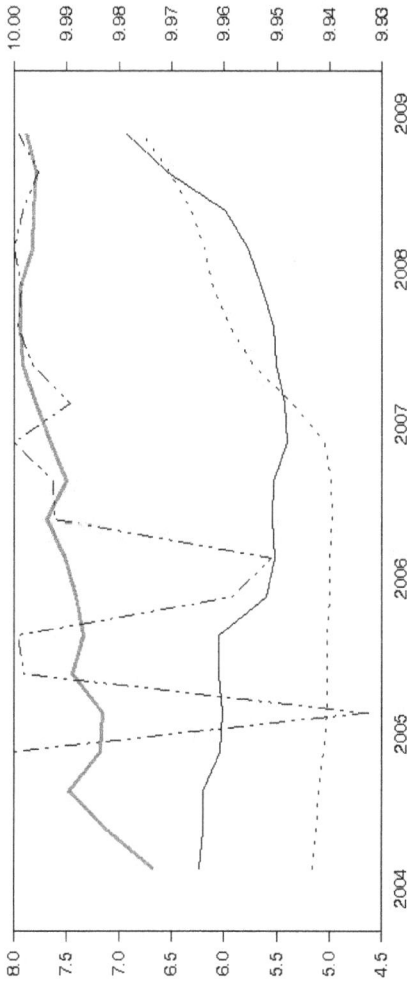

Notes: 1. Authorized approach = solid line (left scale)
2. Normal approach = dotted line (left scale)
3. Direct guarantee = bold heavy line (left scale)
4. Package credit guarantee = half-dotted line (right scale)

Sources: TEJ (Taiwan Economic Journal Co. Ltd.); Directorate-General of Budget, Accounting and Statistics, Executive Yuan, R.O.C. (Taiwan); and Financial Supervisory Commission, Executive Yuan, R.O.C. (Taiwan).

FIGURE 6.6
Effects of SME Loan Guarantees, 2005–09

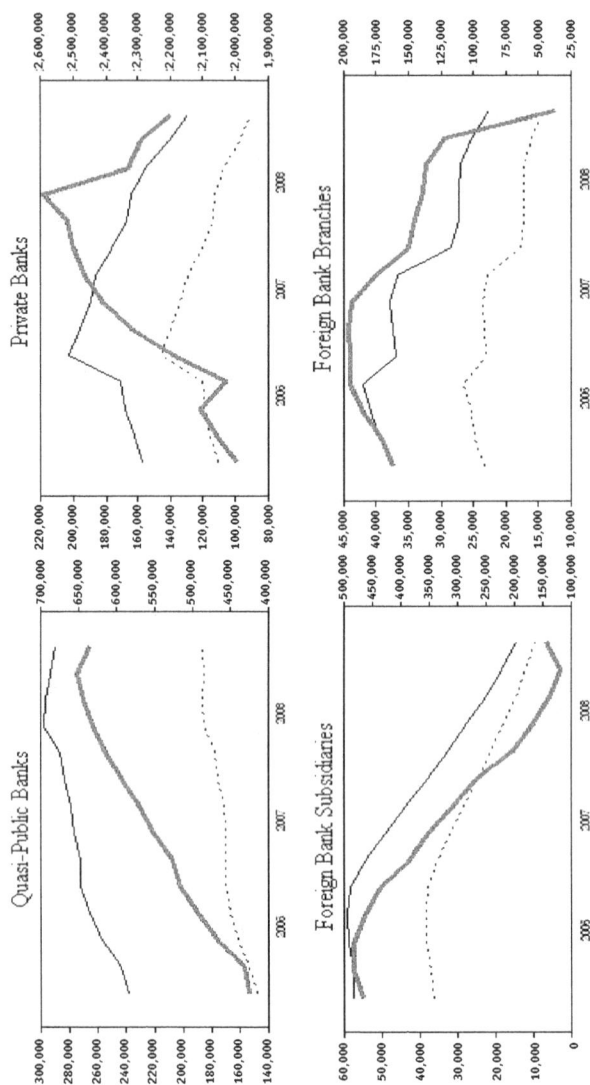

Quasi-Public Banks

Private Banks

Foreign Bank Subsidiaries

Foreign Bank Branches

Notes: 1. Loans to SME = bold solid line (right scale)
2. Loan Guarantee Application = solid line (left scale)
3. Loan Guarantee Approval = dotted line (left scale)

Sources: TEJ (Taiwan Economic Journal Co. Ltd.); Directorate-General of Budget, Accounting and Statistics, Executive Yuan, R.O.C. (Taiwan); and Financial Supervisory Commission, Executive Yuan, R.O.C. (Taiwan).

in the private sector, loans to SMEs have been decreasing even faster for other private enterprises. The Taiwan Government has been trying to help the economy recover by proposing several short-, middle-, and long-term policies.

One of the most important short-term policies has been the support of SME borrowing. The Taiwan SMEG has raised the guaranteed coverage ratios for SMEs whenever banks are willing to lend money to SMEs. This alleviates the problem of decreased lending to some extent. Without raising the guaranteed coverage ratios for SMEs, loans to SMEs may have fallen even more. However, since most manufacturing SMEs have moved to China, loans to SMEs provide limited help for the economy.

During the crisis in 2007–08, foreign banks (including foreign bank subsidiaries and foreign controlling banks) reduced their lending to SMEs faster than state-owned banks and private banks. This suggests some cherry-picking by foreign banks.

Appendix A
Four Types of Banks

The quasi-government banks include: Chang Hwa Bank, First Commercial Bank, Hua Nan Commercial Bank, Mega International Commercial Bank, Taiwan Business Bank, Bank of Kaohsiung, Taiwan Cooperative Bank, Land Bank, and Bank of Taiwan.

The private banks are China Development Industrial Bank, King's Town Bank, Taichung Bank, Chinatrust Commercial Bank, Cathay United Bank, Taipei Fubon Bank, Union Bank, Bank SinoPac, E. SUN Bank, Yuanta Commercial Bank, Taishin Bank, Far Eastern International Bank, Entie Commercial Bank, CHINFON Bank, Taiwan Shin Kong Commercial Bank, SUNNY Bank, The Shanghai Commercial & Savings Bank, HWATAI Bank, COTA Commercial Bank, and Bank of Panhsin.

The foreign bank subsidaries include: Standard and Chartered Bank, Citibank Taiwan, ABN AMRO Bank, The Hongkong and Shanghai Banking Corporation, and DBS Bank.

The foreign controlling banks are: Cosmos Bank, TC Bank, Jih Sun International Bank.

REFERENCES

Beck, T.L., A. Demirgüç-Kunt, and V. Maksimovic. "Bank Competition and Access to Finance". *Journal of Money, Credit and Banking* 36 (2004): 627–48.

Beck, T.L., L. Klapper, and J.C. Mendoza. "The Typology of Partial Credit Guarantee". World Bank Policy Research Working Paper no. 4771, 2008.

Shen, C.H. "Credit-Rationing for Bad Companies in Bad Years: Evidence from Bank Loan Transaction Data". *International Journal of Finance and Economics* 7, no. 3 (2002): 261–78.

7
The Foreign Exchange Crisis in Korea

Shin Jang-Sup

Introduction

The South Korean economy faced a foreign exchange (FX) crisis again during the global financial crisis in 2008–09, a decade after it suffered from a similar disaster during the Asian Financial Crisis in 1997–98. For four months after the collapse of Lehman Brothers in September 2008, Korea saw a massive net outflow amounting to US$46.5 billion of loans held by banks, including domestic banks and foreign bank branches in Korea. The Korean economy virtually came to a "sudden stop" during the period (Rhee 2009).

This time around, Korea avoided seeking a rescue package from the International Monetary Fund (IMF), but survived the crisis thanks to the supply of foreign exchange and credit lines provided by emergency currency swap agreements with the United States, Japan, and China, totalling about US$80 billion. As the crisis was unfolding, the Korean won depreciated sharply, with the KRW-USD rate, which started at 937 in January 2008, rising to 1,200 at the end of September, and further shooting up to 1,500 towards the end of November 2008. It in fact depreciated even more than the currencies of Eastern European countries which actually received the IMF emergency rescue packages.

This Korean experience is puzzling, especially in view of the conventional perception that the country underwent one of the most successful IMF-sponsored reforms after the 1997–98 crisis and achieved "financial stability". The debt-equity ratio of its corporate sector, which was over 400 per cent in 1997, was reduced to about 80 per cent in 2008, even lower than that of the United States. Its public finance was one the soundest among the OECD countries. Its FX reserves, nearly depleted in 1997, ballooned to US$240 billion at the beginning of 2008, making the country the sixth largest holder of foreign reserves in the world. The post-1998 Korean economy boasted "strong fundamentals" and it had hardly been expected that the country would face an FX crisis again.

This chapter investigates the causes of the crisis and discusses policy implications for Korea and other emerging market economies. It pays attention to the fact that the Korean economy actually became more vulnerable to abrupt international capital flows after the IMF-sponsored reforms. This weakness was not visible when international capital kept flowing into Korea during the first half of 2000s but became evident with the deepening of the global financial crisis in 2008–09. The chapter therefore suggests shifting its economic system to one that can better control capital flows and stabilize its FX rates.

Reassessing the "Successful" IMF Programme

The IMF programme instituted in Korea after the 1997–98 crisis consisted of three elements: (1) macroeconomic retrenchment, (2) market opening, and (3) structural reforms (for details, see Table 7.1). Let us put aside macroeconomic retrenchment because it was a shock therapy at the beginning of the crisis and was reversed in the middle of 1998. Let us focus on market opening and structural reforms to assess long-term effects of the programme.

In this programme, it is important to note that the market is depicted as a stabilizing force whereas the government is regarded as a destabilizing force. This is why market opening and structural reforms are combined as measures to prevent future financial crises. Therefore, a fuller liberalization of product and capital markets was undertaken while "rigidities" of the economy introduced by government interventions were minimized. All trade-related subsidies were abolished and remaining import barriers were removed. The foreign exchange rate system was changed to a free floating system by abolishing the daily exchange rate band and limiting government's intervention in the FX market. The upper limit to foreigners' domestic shareholding was also eliminated, the bond market fully opened, and commercial lending further liberalized. As far as market openness is concerned, Korea became a full First World country after the crisis.

At the same time, four major system reforms were carried out to address the alleged "structural problems" that made the economy vulnerable to a financial crisis. In the financial sector, it was thought that the most serious structural

TABLE 7.1
Major Components of the IMF Programme in Korea

Category	Subcategory	Contents
Retrenchment	Monetary Policy	— increase call rates and reduce the M3 growth rate
	Budgetary Policy	— maintain a small budget surplus (the 1ˢᵗ MOU)
Market Opening	Product Market	— remove trade-related subsidies
		— import liberalization of remaining items
	Capital Market	— abolish daily exchange rate band and limit intervention in the FX market
		— remove restrictions on foreign ownership of equities and real estates
		— full liberalization of the bond market
		— remove remaining restrictions on foreign borrowings by corporations and financial institutions

continued on next page

TABLE 7.1 — *cont'd*

Category	Subcategory	Contents
Four System Reforms	Financial Sector	— strengthen financial supervision
		— disposal of insolvent financial institutions
		— strengthening governance of financial institutions
	Corporate Sector	— reduce debt-equity ratio
		— liberalize M&A market
		— introduce consolidated financial statement
		— strengthen right of minority shareholders
	Labour Market	— make redundancy layoffs easier
		— legalize "dispatch labour"
	Public Sector	— privatize public enterprises
		— reduce government regulations drastically

Source: Shin and Chang (2003).

problem lay in the supervision and monitoring system. So a Financial Supervisory Commission was launched as the agency for the comprehensive supervision of financial institutions. Supervision standards were tightened by applying the BIS (Bank for International Settlements) capital adequacy ratio and so on. The governance of financial institutions was reformed by introducing the external board system in which a significant number of non-executive directors took part in decision-making. The government also closed many non-viable commercial banks and non-bank financial institutions (NBFIs), and forced mergers and acquisitions (M&As).

In the corporate sector, the *chaebol* structure became the major target of reform because it was accused of being the cause of "over-expansion without accountability" that led to the crisis. The *chaebol* were made to reduce radically their debt-equity ratios, which rose far above 400 per cent at the end of 1997 to 200 per cent in less than two years. Loan guarantees and internal transactions among the *chaebol* affiliate firms were prohibited. The *chaebol* were also requested to concentrate on "core" businesses by selling, closing, and swapping "peripheral" businesses. The reform of corporate governance was particularly predicated on the perception that the "dictatorial" management by "owner" families was the root cause of their "reckless" expansion and the consequent national financial crisis.

The labour market was also "reformed" supposedly to increase its "flexibility" despite the fact that Korea already has one of the most flexible labour markets among the OECD countries. Even before the crisis, it has the highest ratio of temporary workers in the workforce among the

OECD countries (Crotty and Lee 2001). Following the agreement with the IMF, the Korean National Assembly passed a law that made redundancy layoff easier. "Dispatch labour", that is, employing temporary workers recruited through specialized agencies, was also legalized. As part of the public sector reforms, the existing privatization plan of major public enterprises was strengthened while new plans were added. Government regulations for industries were also drastically reduced.

In a nutshell, the IMF programme was directed at remoulding the Korean economy in the idealized image of the Anglo-American system, in keeping up with "global standards". External liberalization progressed in full. The role of the government was confined to supervising financial institutions and maintaining competitive market order. In this programme, liberalization is "untouchable" and the only way open to crisis-hit countries to achieve financial stability was to strengthen what the IMF considered internal "fundamentals" of the economy. The blame of falling into a financial crisis was wholly on the shoulder of crisis-hit countries, not the international financial market.

Korea probably became the country implementing this prescription most faithfully in IMF history. For instance, Korea attained IMF's target of obtaining a lower than 200 per cent of corporate debt-equity ratio far ahead of the original plan, and further reduced this to around 80 per cent in 2007, even lower than that of the United States which was over 100 per cent that year. Korea's commercial banks also improved their financial standing. Their BIS ratio, which was less than 4 per cent on the eve of the 1997 crisis, rose to 10 per cent in 1999 and then to 12 per cent at the beginning of 2008.

The Global Financial Crisis and Capital Flight from Korea

Korea's experience during the 2008–09 global financial crisis goes against the basic tenet of the IMF programme. For it was not its internal "structural problems" that destabilized the economy, but the international financial market that was supposed to provide a stabilizing force to the economy which drove the country to experience another FX crisis. Korea became a victim of the financial crisis even though it had addressed those structural problems most "successfully" after the 1997–98 crisis.

Table 7.2 shows who are responsible for Korea's FX crisis during the global financial crisis. One major factor

TABLE 7.2
Korea's Capital Account during the
Global Financial Crisis, 2008

Unit: US$ billions

	Jan–Aug 2008	*Sept–Dec 2008*
Net borrowings	18.2	–46.5
Equities	–34.9	0.0
(Residents)	–2.9	9.3
(Non-residents)	–32.0	–9.3
Bonds	21.5	–1.9
(Residents)	3.8	13.0
(Non-residents)	17.7	–14.9
Direct investment	–9.7	–0.9
Others	0.2	3.2
Total	–4.7	–46.2

Source: Rhee (2009).

that depressed the Korean won was the continued withdrawal of money by foreign investors during the process of global deleveraging brought on by the worsening of the subprime crisis. During the first eight months of 2008 before the collapse of Lehman Brothers, foreign investors took US$32 billion net out from the Korean stock market. In total, foreign investors sold more than 60 trillion won (about US$60 billion) of Korean stocks for one year up to the Lehman collapse, which amounted to about a quarter of Korea's foreign reserves. The foreign share of the Korean stock market, which used to be one of the highest in the world at about 40 per cent in 2006, dropped sharply to about 28 per cent in September 2008.

On top of this, there was a "run" in the banking sector after the Lehman collapse. The loan withdrawal from the banking sector amounted to US$46.5 billion in net value in the last four months of 2008, although the withdrawal of funds from the equity market was stabilized. According to the Bank of Korea, about half of the withdrawals was made by foreign banks' branches in Korea. Foreign banks justified this massive transfer of funds in time of the crisis by saying it was a "capital hedge", meaning that they were adjusting their global portfolio in view of the possible reduction in value of assets held in Korean won in their branches because it was highly likely that the Korean won would depreciate further with the Lehman collapse. However, it was also possible that they had speculated on the depreciation of Korean won actually and realized it by moving their money out of Korea when its currency looked precarious. Whether the transfer had to do with capital hedge or currency speculation, it dealt a blow to the Korean economy which had already suffered from a continued outflow of money with global deleveraging.

The remainder of the net outflow from the banking sector in the last four months of 2008 was from domestic banks as their revolving short-term foreign loans were not extended. Even this amount cannot be considered entirely their fault. Foreign banks were deleveraging their portfolios to respond to the liquidity crunch caused by the subprime crisis and many of them also came to a "sudden stop" in their home countries after the collapse of Lehman Brothers and were not able to extend credit to other banks. If we suppose that domestic banks and foreign banks were each half and half responsible for loan amount not extended, we can say that foreign banks were responsible for three quarters of the US$46.5 billion net outflow from the banking sector after the Lehman collapse. Before the Lehman collapse in September, foreign investors took their money out of the Korean equity market mostly because they needed cash for deleveraging, not because they thought the Korea market prospect was particularly bleak. Considering these circumstances, it is safe to say that the FX crisis in Korea in 2008 was basically created by foreign investors and banks, not by the Korean economy itself.

This situation was very different from the one in 1997 when Korea went under the IMF stewardship. At that time, the outflow of money was mostly from domestic banks which provided Korean corporations with loans by borrowing money from foreign banks, or directly from domestic corporations that had built up debt obligations with foreign banks. Even in this case, it is debatable whether the Korean economy was entirely at fault because the contagion from the Southeast Asian financial crisis and "panic" and/or speculation by international investors and banks also contributed to the crisis. If sources of money flowing out of Korea are as we considered above, it is difficult to say that the FX crisis in 2008 was due to problems in the Korean economy. It is better understood as a result of "capital flight" by foreign investors and foreign banks.

Why was the Korean Economy so Susceptible to the FX Crisis?

The IMF programme had supposed that crisis-hit countries had structural problems and the international financial market was a judge that ultimately determines the "soundness" of countries by voting with their feet and taking money into the ones with good fundamentals while pulling out money from the ones with unsound fundamentals. Therefore, its structural reforms are entirely directed at crisis-hit countries, not at the international financial market. In fact, the international market was given much more freedom than crisis-hit countries through various liberalization and reform measures. However, the Korean experience during the global crisis has turned this conventional view upside down. Korea had a crisis even with its strong fundamentals. It looks more likely now that it was the international financial market that had structural problems of creating and busting bubbles, and Korea became a victim of these vicissitudes.

It seems to me this is a more general case for a financial crisis, considering the historical fact that capitalism has been progressing with boom and bust cycles, and the recent experience shows international financial crises became more frequent with the liberalization of the global financial market from the 1980s. If one follows through this direction of thought, it is better to find "structural causes" from reasons that made it difficult for an individual country to shield its economy from the instability of the international financial market rather than from its internal problems. We should also be cautious in determining what is "structural" and what is not. They can be determined only after examining the causes at the level of individual countries. Structural ones are those more durable and more important for a certain country for a certain period. We cannot predetermine structural causes for any country or any period. I will analyse below causes of the 2008–09 FX crisis in Korea in this spirit.

One visible weakness of the Korean economy during the global financial crisis lay in its capital market structure that made it a "cash dispenser" for foreign investors in the process of global deleveraging. The foreign share of stock in Korea was one of the highest in the world, increasing from 13 per cent in 1996 to 42 per cent in 2004. Although foreign investors reduced their share from the peak in 2004, it was still about 38 per cent before the beginning of the global deleveraging in September 2007 (see Figure 7.1). This level was still one of the highest in the world. For instance, at the end of 2003, the foreign share in the domestic stock market was 38.8 per cent in France, 32.1 per cent in the United Kingdom, 28.7 per cent in Australia, 17.7 per cent in Japan, 15.0 per cent in Germany, and 10.3 per cent in the United States, respectively, while that of Korea was 40.1 per cent (Kim 2006).

For foreign investors who had to cash out from their existing global portfolios to deleverage, a priority was given to markets where they had capital gains and which provided

FIGURE 7.1
Foreign Share of Listed Korean Stocks, 1994–2008
(value, %)

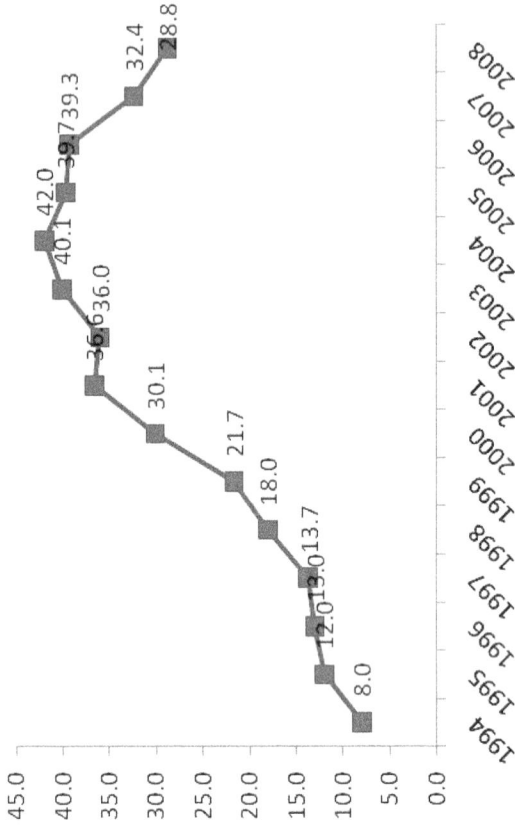

Source: Korea Stock Exchange.

sufficient liquidity. Unfortunately for Korea, its stock market met these two conditions. Foreign investors had hefty paper gains from their investment because the Korean stock market kept rising when they increased their shares in the 2000s. On top of this, they also enjoyed FX gains because the Korean won kept strengthening until the middle of 2007. Moreover, the Korean stock market was the biggest and most liquid among emerging markets. Foreign investors suddenly reduced their share by more than 10 percentage points in the one year leading up to the collapse of Lehman Brothers. This was not because they thought the outlook of the Korean economy particularly bleak, but because the Korean market was one of the most convenient places to sell their assets for deleveraging.

The situation was exacerbated by speculative activities by foreign investors. Once it became clear that massive sell-out would happen in the Korean market, they had every reason to bet on the depreciation of the Korean won. As long as global deleveraging was going on, there was not much chance that the Korean won would appreciate. For currency speculators, it was a game they hardly lose to bet against the Korean won.

Moreover, this kind of currency speculation became a much easier and safer bet because Korea had completed its capital account liberalization as a result of the IMF programme and the government was committed to the free movement of capital and a free floating FX system for its agenda to develop the country as a financial hub of the region. For currency speculators, there was little policy risk because it was unlikely that the Korean Government would reverse its policy stance. By anticipating further withdrawals of money, many foreign investors shorted both Korean stocks and Korean won together. According to the Financial Supervisory Service, the amount of short-selling on Korean stocks, mostly done by foreign investors, exceeded 30 trillion won (about US$30 billion) for the first nine months of 2008, and about 10 trillion won of these transactions were illegal.[1] However, the Korean authorities did not really deal with the speculation, whether legal or illegal.

Korea had another weakness that made it vulnerable to currency speculation. Its import structure is rigid and susceptible to commodity price shocks because raw materials account for more than half of its total import bill even in time of stable prices, and comprises about half of these imported raw materials. If commodity prices increase sharply, the total import bill suddenly swells, tilting Korea's current account balance easily into a deficit.

When the global deleveraging was going on in 2008, commodity market bubbles grew rapidly, especially in the oil sector. Crude oil price (WTI), which stood at US$72 per barrel in August 2007, rose to over US$100 per barrel in February 2008 and further to US$133 per barrel in July 2008. It was during this period that Goldman Sachs released a report forecasting that crude oil price would hit US$200 per barrel in 2009, fuelling speculation on oil. Due to the rise in commodity prices, Korea's import of raw materials increased from US$173.9 billion in 2006 to US$201.7 billion in 2007 and further to US$268.6 billion in 2008. The share of raw materials in the total import bill, therefore, rose from 56.5 per cent in 2007 to 61.7 per cent in 2008. Korea's current account, which had shown a surplus throughout the 2000s, showed a deficit from December 2007 and its size continued to rise until August 2008. As Figure 7.2 shows, Korea's monthly current account deficit is closely related to commodity prices, especially oil prices.

This posed a dilemma for Korea's FX policy. The increase in current account deficit points to a depreciation of the Korean won, whereas the increase in import prices of raw materials pushes the government to intervene in the FX market to contain the depreciation of the won in an attempt to ease the pressure on domestic prices. For currency speculators who had already bet on the depreciation of the won following global deleveraging, this policy dilemma provided another incentive to bet even more against the Korean won because it was almost certain that the government's intervention in the FX market would be short-lived and the speculators could gain more profits by utilizing the intervention. To save its foreign reserves holding, the Korean Government intervened in derivative markets. But it lost 6.3 trillion won (about US$55 billion) by the end of 2008 from its Exchange Stabilisation Fund.[2] This huge loss to the government was a gain to those who speculated against the Korean won.

During the Korean crisis, the attention of foreign analysts and the media was focused on Korea's short-term foreign debts. The Korean Government was also active in defending its FX position related to short-term debts. There was actually a rapid increase in short-term foreign debts before the unfolding of the global financial crisis and it would be natural to think that this build-up of short-term debts was responsible for the FX crisis. Short-term debts held by the banking sector increased from US$44.5 billion in 2004 to US$96.1 billion in 2006, and then to US$134.0 billion in

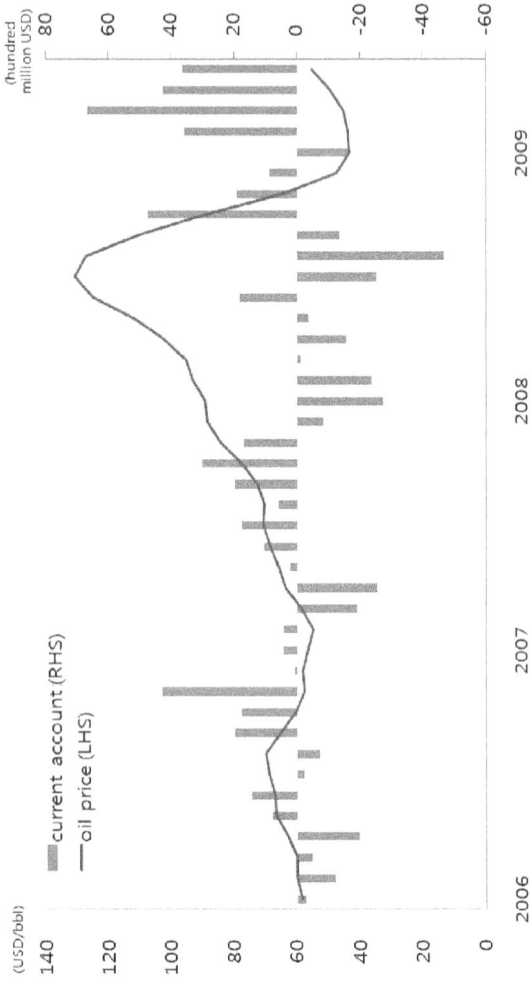

FIGURE 7.2
Oil Price and Current Account of Korea
(January 2006–May 2009)

Source: Rhee (2009).

2007. Total short-term debts also rose from US$50.8 billion in 2004, to US$113.7 billion in 2006, and then US$160.2 billion in 2007 (see Figure 7.3).

If one examines the make-up of the short-term foreign debts, however, one would see that these debts were not really serious, especially when one looks at these confined to domestic banks. The Korean Government had controlled the short-term debt position of its commercial banks quite tightly because it had diagnosed that the rapid build-up of short-term debts in the middle of the 1990s was a major factor contributing to the 1997–98 financial crisis. In its attempts to achieve financial stability, the Korean financial authorities had made it nearly compulsory for domestic banks to square their positions when they increase their short-term foreign debts by simultaneously increasing their foreign currency-denominated assets. Therefore, the FX position (foreign assets minus foreign liabilities) of domestic banks was almost squared: as of August 2008, just before the Lehman collapse, their external debts were US$173.3 billion while their external assets were US$165.8 billion, leaving only a US$7.5-billion shortfall. Over 90 per cent of the total shortfall of US$67.6 billion was due to the position of foreign bank branches in Korea, which held US$100.5 billion of foreign debts and US$ 40.4 billion of foreign assets (Rhee 2009).

Korean regulators were lenient to the unmatched position of foreign bank branches for mainly two reasons. First, in its attempt to develop Korea as a regional financial hub, they wanted to ensure free flow of capital and attract more foreign banks to Korea through deregulation. Second, they had hardly thought of the possibility that foreign banks

FIGURE 7.3
Trend of Korea's Short-term Foreign Debts

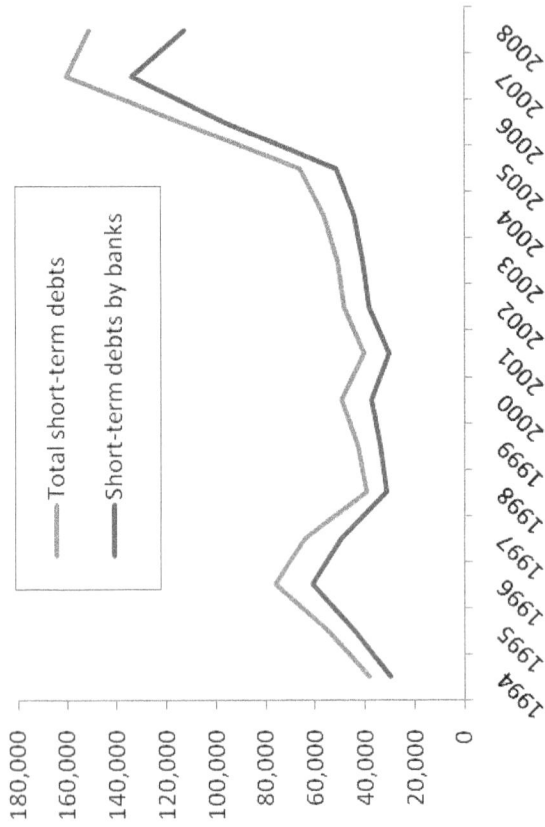

Source: The Bank of Korea.

would cause a foreign liquidity crisis in Korea. On the contrary, they had thought that the presence of foreign banks on a bigger scale would protect the Korean economy from a possible FX crisis because their assets were mostly held in foreign currencies and their main offices were powerful enough to help their branches in times of crisis. When the Financial Services Commission (2008) explained Korea's foreign reserves position to international investors during the crisis, it therefore emphasized the fact that its foreign reserves were more than sufficient to cover short-term debts held by domestic banks, and it did not consider those held by foreign bank branches as an issue the Korean Government should worry about. As Figure 7.4 shows, of the US$175.7 billion of short-term debts, domestic banks only held US$85.4 billion (48.6 per cent) and their foreign reserves were enough to cover any problems arising from this. However, contrary to expectations, foreign bank branches became the main source of capital flight after the Lehman collapse, as pointed out above. A main regulatory hole of the Korean economy before and during the crisis lay in cross-border capital flows of foreign bank branches, not domestic banks.

What Should Be Done Next?

Even though Korea experienced this second FX crisis, its policy responses were more or less the same as before. Capital market liberalization was still "untouchable" and policy efforts were again only directed at strengthening domestic fundamentals. The Financial Services Commission unveiled in November 2009 its "new" regulations as follows:

FIGURE 7.4
Composition of Korea's Foreign Debt
(US$ billions, as of October 2008)

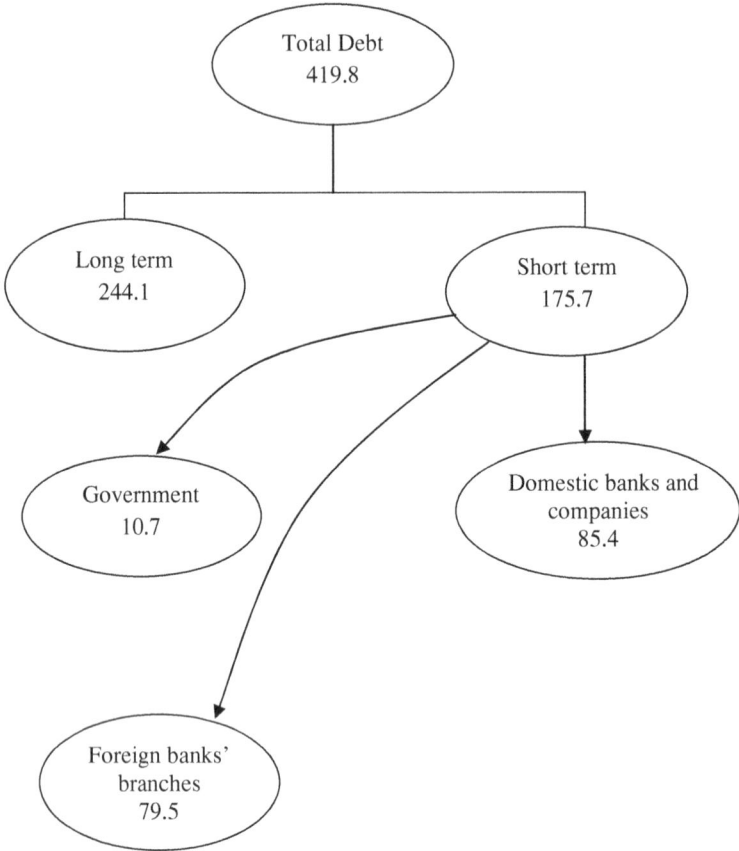

Source: Financial Services Commission (2008).

(1) tightening regulations to increase mid- to long-term financing in foreign loan portfolios, (2) strengthening regulations on FX liquidity ratio and liquidity risk management, (3) introducing mandatory minimum holdings of safe FX assets, (4) introducing new standards for FX derivatives trading and risk management, and so on. However, they were only applied to domestic banks. The Commission clearly stated that "Meanwhile, foreign bank branches are only subject to risk management standards on FX derivatives transactions and reporting obligation; they will not be subject to liquidity ratio regulations and other direct regulations" (Financial Services Commission 2009).

Considering the causes of the FX crisis discussed above, the exemption of foreign bank branches from most of the new regulations is most baffling. They were the main culprits of the "sudden stop" phenomenon after the Lehman collapse. Yet they are still allowed to operate in Korea as freely as before despite the harm they did to the Korean economy. One major reason behind this decision had to do with the Korean Government's commitment to free capital flows and its emphasis on coordinating policies with G20 countries. It was hesitant to introduce regulations that may harm its newly earned credential of a free market economy. As an active and even leading participant of G20 meetings, it was also reluctant to introduce new regulations on international capital flows ahead of other G20 countries.

The policy choice of the Korean Government in effect only provided lip service to reducing the country's financial vulnerability because pursuing its goal of developing the economy as a financial hub and/or playing a leading role in G20 was given higher priority. For instance, the effect of tightening regulations on the short-term debts of domestic banks to decrease financial risks to the economy is dubious. Korea's short-term to total debt ratio was 39.7 per cent at the end of 2008, lower than that of Britain (74.4 per cent), Hong Kong (73.3 per cent), Switzerland (69.9 per cent), Japan (62.5 per cent), Ireland (48.0 per cent), France (42.8 per cent), or Canada (40.2 per cent). Korea's short-term debt to foreign reserves ratio was also one of the lowest among G20 countries at 75.1 per cent at the end of 2008. The ratio was much higher in Ireland (107,019.3 per cent), Britain (10,657.5 per cent), the United States (6,911.9 per cent), France (2,077.7 per cent), Canada (687.7 per cent), Japan (142.3 per cent), to cite some prominent examples.

Moreover, Brazil and Russia also experienced FX crises during the global financial crisis even though they had short-term to total debt ratios (13.9 per cent and 16.5 per cent, respectively) that were and short-term to foreign reserves ratios (18.8 per cent and 18.7 per cent, respectively) that were even lower than those of Korea.[3] If an FX crisis occurred due to the loss of confidence in the countries concerned, their management of short-term debts could be an important issue. If an FX crisis happened due to external factors such as global deleveraging, however, the size of short-term debts could not be a central issue. Foreign investors and banks pulled their money out mainly to address their own liquidity problems, and in the process, created FX crises to countries that happened to have high foreign holdings and a liberal capital account regime.

For the Korean Government, at least for the current administration, the effectiveness of financial regulations was given secondary priority, and overshadowed by that given to building a financial hub or playing a leading role in G20. However, a more fundamental reconsideration of policy priorities seem to be necessary. For instance, it should be asked whether it is really desirable and feasible to develop the country as a regional financial hub. If so, it should be also asked whether this can be done only by allowing free capital flows and introducing more foreign capital, leaving the economy vulnerable to external shocks. Similarly, it should be asked whether Korea could play a leading role in G20 by advocating free capital flows. It is possible that the country could play a more important role by advocating regulatory measures that would help shield individual countries from the instability of FX rate movements and international capital flows.

If the priority of policy is to be given to the achievement of financial stability itself, it goes without saying that the government should deal with major causes of the FX crisis directly, rather than only dealing with minor ones. As analysed above, capital flights by foreign investors and foreign banks were a major cause of the FX crisis in Korea, and internal fundamentals, including a rapid increase in short-term debts, were a minor one. It is then necessary to introduce policy measures to control capital flows and reduce their destabilizing impact on the economy.

I have suggested an introduction of "selective capital controls" and a change of the FX system to a basket system for Korea in this respect. I will only briefly sketch the outline of these here (Shin 2009). The starting point of the policy suggestion is the abandonment of the myth of "fundamentals". Korea experienced a financial crisis again despite having one of the best set of "fundamentals" among OECD countries. This is mainly because international capital flows and FX rates are not really determined by those fundamentals. For instance, global FX trading volume hit more than US$800 trillion in 2007 and, of this, less than 3 per cent can be attributed to those related to the real economy as the world trading volume was just over US$12 trillion in 2007. This gap still continues to increase and FX trading volume is estimated to reach over US$1,000 trillion in 2009. We should accept that a chronic discrepancy between market FX rates and fundamentals is an undeniable fact in the global financial market. It is then unrealistic to expect that market FX rates would align with the needs of the real economy. So it is necessary for the government to introduce a system that can reduce the gap and help smooth working of the real economy. Fixed FX systems, which fix the rate to the movement of an international currency, for instance, the U.S. dollar, put undue pressure of adjustment on the real economy because the value of the anchor currency also changes against other currencies. A basket system is more recommendable as a middle-of-the-road system which allows changes of FX rates to follow those among major trading and investment partners, while the government has a controlling power over the market in determining FX rates.

If an FX system moves away from the free floating system, it is necessary to introduce capital controls because of the "impossible trinity", that is, a fixed FX system, free capital flows, and monetary autonomy cannot be achieved simultaneously (Mundell 1968). To maintain monetary autonomy in order to be able to adjust monetary supply to the changing needs of the domestic economy, it is necessary to control capital flows if the country also wants to regulate FX rates. In the case of Korea, foreign investors and banks pulled out funds amounting to a quarter of Korea's foreign reserves in one year. If an economy is exposed to this kind of abrupt capital outflows, it cannot expect to maintain financial stability, especially when external conditions become volatile and therefore the need to secure stability is more acute.

Conclusion

In contemplating policy measures to counter financial crises, it is important to acknowledge the fact that globalization is Janus-faced: globalization promises bigger markets and more competition to achieve higher economic growth and efficiency through freer movement of products and services across national borders, but it also increases financial instability through larger and more volatile cross-border capital flows. At the beginning of the accelerated globalization from the 1980s, academics and policy-makers were more concerned with the bright side of globalization, which would open great opportunities for a country to grow faster by utilizing a greater availability of resources and markets.

However, globalization came with high costs, in particular, with the growing incidence of financial crises. According to Eichengreen and Bordo (2002), the number of financial crises increased from 21 between 1945–71 to 44 between 1971 and 1997 for industrial countries, and from 17 between 1945 and 1971 to 95 between 1971 and 1997 for emerging markets. Between 1971 and 1997, a randomly selected country had as high as a 10–12 per cent probability of experiencing a financial crisis.

On the whole, the economic performance of the world economy during the period of accelerated globalization is far from encouraging. Per capita income growth rate in the world economy actually decelerated as the pace of globalization accelerated and this trend was more marked in developing countries than in developed countries. The per capita income growth rate of the world fell from 2.7 per cent in the period 1961–80 to 1.2 per cent in the period 1980–99. For the same periods of comparison, the figure for developing countries fell from 3.2 per cent to 1.5 per cent while that for developed countries decreased from 3.6 per cent to 2.0 per cent. This was mainly because financial crises themselves reduced growth rates on the one hand, and on the other, the maintenance of conservative macroeconomic regime for fear of possible financial crises constrained economies from further expansion.

The global financial crisis is a costly reminder of the dark side of globalization. Korea's financial regulatory regime, which was completed after it implemented the IMF programme, was based only on the bright aspects of globalization and showed full confidence in the international financial market. The experience of Korea as well as other countries during the global financial crisis demonstrates the pitfalls of this market fundamentalism. The state should be brought back to ensure stable growth and regulate the instability of the market.

NOTES

1. *Korea Economic Daily*, 18 September 2008.
2. *The Maeil Business News*, 7 September 2009.
3. SERI (2009, table in appendix).

REFERENCES

Crotty, James and Lee Kang-Kook. "Economic Performance in Post-Crisis Korea: A Critical Perspective on Neoliberal Restructuring". Mimeographed, 2001.

Financial Services Commission. *The Korean Financial Market and Economy: Resilience Amidst Turbulence*. 2008.

———. *Supervision of Financial Institutions' FX Soundness Strengthened*. 2009.

Kim, Yang-Soo. Auditing Financial and Economic Committee, National Assembly of Korea (in Korean). 2006.

Mundell, Robert. *International Economics*. New York: Macmillan, 1968.

Rhee, Gwang-Ju. "Foreign Exchange Liquidity Pressures in Korea: Recent Experience and Lessons". Paper presented at "The 2009 KDI-JEP Conference on Financial Crisis, Recovery and Sustaining Growth". Seoul, Korea, 2009.

Samsung Economic Research Institute. "Assessment of the Foreign Debt Structure of Korea and Suggestions to Improve It". Issue Paper 10, August 2009.

Shin, Jang-Sup. *The Five Theorems on the Financial Crisis and the Design of the Korean Economy* (in Korean). Seoul: Cheonglim, 2009.

Shin, Jang-Sup and Ha-Joon Chang. *Restructuring Korea Inc.: Financial Crisis, Corporate Reform, and Institutional Transition*. London: Routledge, 2003.

8
Global Financial Crisis and Policy Issues in Japan

Naoyuki Yoshino

Why Do Bubbles Occur?

Japan experienced an asset bubble in the late 1980s when stock and land prices roughly tripled in a matter of several years before plunging to their original levels — that is, one third of their peak values — following the burst of the bubble (see Figure 8.1). Japanese banks, which typically accept land as collateral for loans, went on a lending spree when land prices were on the rise because the higher land prices boosted collateral values. The banks had become more lenient in their attitudes towards lending as prices were going up, but when land prices eventually headed back down, the same banks tightened their credit standards to such an extent that it caused a "credit crunch". Land price declines from 1991 onwards leading to a deterioration of corporate business performance and forced many corporate borrowers to default on their loan repayments, which resulted in a massive accumulation of non-performing loans on the banks' balance sheets.

FIGURE 8.1
Japanese Banks, Stock Prices and Land Prices, 1983–2006

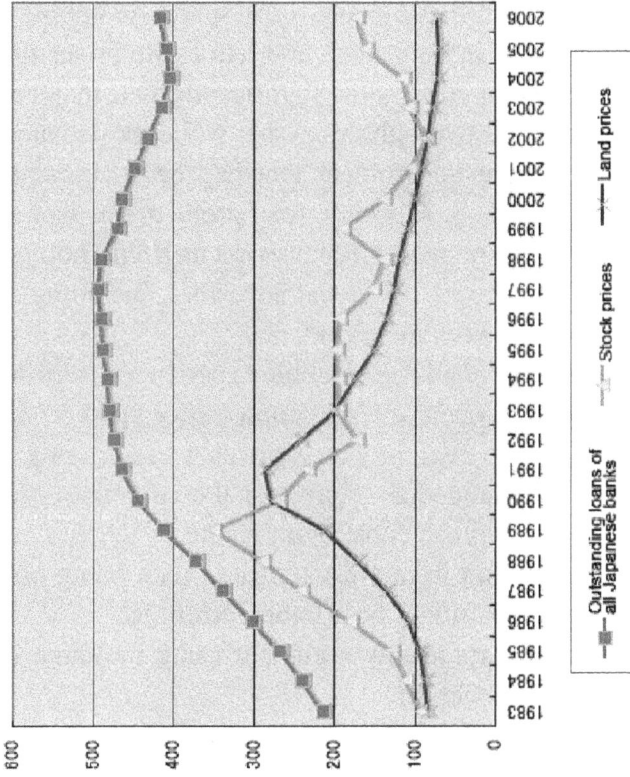

Legend: Outstanding loans of all Japanese banks — Stock prices — Land prices

Despite Japan's painful bubble experience, South Korea went through its own bubble ordeal when property values shot up in 2005 before also falling off the cliff. In China, likewise, Shanghai stock prices had surged until December 2007, then abruptly fell to around one third of their peak level by October 2008. As was the case in post-bubble Japan, the collapse of the U.S. subprime bubble triggered steep drops in both stock and real estate prices that caused the real economy to slow significantly. One major difference between the two bubbles is that while the Japanese bubble was a domestic problem that had been contained within Japan, the U.S. subprime loan problem has had an impact on the entire world because securitized mortgage loans were purchased by global investors, including banks, in countries across the world.

In spite of all these bubble experiences, why do bubbles continue to occur in one country after another? In autumn 2006, when real property prices were soaring in South Korea, I attended an international conference organized by the South Korean construction industry where I argued that the escalation in real estate prices then being observed in South Korea might be a bubble forming.

I will explain my argument using the three indicators shown in Table 8.1.

When I visited South Korea and China in the midst of their bubbles, I compared each situation to the Japanese bubble in the late 1980s using the data in Table 8.1 and various monetary policy indicators. In both countries, I explained that their situation, judging from economic indicators, resembled that of Japan in the late 1980s. However, a Chinese scholar refuted my argument on a televised talk show, saying:

TABLE 8.1
Bubble Indicators

(i)   Changes in the ratio of real estate loans to total outstanding bank loans (In Japan, the ratio increased from 16 per cent to 32.6 per cent at the peak of the bubble.)
(ii) Comparison between the growth rates of real estate bank loans and the real economy
(iii) Average income multiple required to buy a house

Source: Author's own observations.

1. China is in a phase comparable to Japan's post-war high-growth period, and the current rise in land and stock prices is not a bubble but reflects economic fundamentals; and thus,
2. The current Chinese situation differs from that of the Japanese bubble, in which the escalation of land and stock prices occurred long after the high-growth period had ended.

In South Korea, I had a similar discussion and my explanation was once again rejected as incorrect. But shortly afterwards, land prices fell in South Korea. Likewise, in the latter half of 2008, Chinese stock prices plunged to a level approximately one third of their peak level.

To be sure, not everyone was so optimistic in China. For instance, Yu Yongding of the Chinese Academy of Social Sciences (CASS) had approached me at quite an early stage for advice on how to stop the Chinese bubble. Several Chinese media outlets also carried my article urging China to stop the bubble. Yet the prevailing argument in China was that tightening monetary policy, a step that could slow the economy, was absolutely not a choice when there was no bubble in the Chinese market.

A bubble economy makes many people feel happy. Higher stock prices lead to an increase in household expenditure because people, feeling richer, begin spending and travelling more. And such spending sprees boost sales for many companies, which in turn expand their capital expenditure. As a result, the economy grows, people's income increases, and everyone is satisfied. If a central bank pre-emptively tightens its grip under these conditions, it is bound to be criticized for throwing the otherwise robust economy into the doldrums and making people's lives worse off. It is thus extremely difficult for a central bank to tighten pre-emptively, even when it concludes that there are signs of a bubble forming. Given this reality, it is anticipated that bubbles will continue to occur in the future.

Global Excess Liquidity

When we look at global capital flows, we can see that China, Japan, and several other countries with current account surpluses have accumulated massive foreign reserves, with a large portion of these reserves held in the form of U.S. treasury securities. This means that funds accumulated by continuously running current account surpluses are being channelled back into the United States, an overly consumptive society with a low savings rate (that is, high consumption rate) and a robust investment rate that is far in excess of savings.

Excess liquidity existed in the United States and Japan because monetary authorities in both countries had taken an accommodative stance to prevent their respective economies from sliding. A typical spending pattern emerged in the United States where households borrowed money to buy homes, and then borrowed more to spend on consumption as home values appreciated. The U.S. subprime loan problem has eloquently demonstrated just how much the availability of excess funds could induce significant growth in mortgage loans to low-income households whose credit risk would have been considered too high in normal conditions.

Overseas financial institutions also took advantage of Japan's zero interest rate policy under which the short-term borrowing rate has been kept virtually at zero. In what has been referred to as the yen carry trade, global investors borrowed yen in Japan and invested in higher-yielding foreign-currency assets elsewhere.

Easing monetary policy is obviously a central bank action required for pushing down interest rates and propping up corporate capital expenditure enough to prevent an economic downturn. Such expansionary monetary policies pursued by the central banks of some major economies, however, led to excess global liquidity that contributed to the recent financial crisis. As discussed above, initially everyone was happy with rising stock prices supported by accommodative monetary policies, and central banks failed to take tightening steps in a timely manner.

A Bubble Bursts When Microeconomic Behaviour Aggregates Into Macroeconomic Behaviour

The U.S. subprime loan phenomenon, or lending to borrowers with less-than-ideal credit records, began when mortgage companies and financial institutions started issuing mortgage loans to undercapitalized, low-income home buyers. In doing so, they had told the borrowers "you can take out a mortgage loan to buy a house, and you will not have any problems paying back the loan because the price of your house is expected to go up enough to cover the principal and interest payments on the loan." The lenders then securitized these mortgage loans and sold them in the market. Credit rating agencies assigned high credit ratings to such securitized loan receivables because they were backed by home mortgages.

Mortgage-backed securities (MBS) soon became very attractive investment vehicles that were purchased by investors not only in the United States, but across the world. At first these activities occurred at a microeconomic level among only a limited number of players and did not have a significant impact on the financial system as a whole. The first group of subprime lenders — that is, housing companies and financial institutions that were the first to offer loans to subprime borrowers — received benefits in the form of improved earnings.

However, after seeing these early subprime lenders reap great profits from subprime loans, many of their competitors followed suit and launched their own securitization schemes. And this eventually aggregated into macroeconomic behaviour. With a large number of mortgage companies doing the same thing, an excess supply of housing started building up, which drove down housing prices, undermined the very foundation on which the achievement of their speculative goal hinged, and eventually led to the near collapse of the entire financial system. This was how the financial crisis unfolded.

Financial Innovation and Regulation

The U.S. financial sector has invented a diverse set of financial tools and technologies. In Japan, a leading non-life insurer once initiated a plan to sell policies insuring against the risk of falling stock prices. But the plan, which would have led to the development of an instrument to hedge against financial risks, failed to materialize because the Ministry of Finance did not give its approval. The ministry denounced the idea of having the risk of stock prices — a risk that should be borne by the investors who bought the stock — covered by another financial instrument.

As evidenced by this anecdote, the Japanese regulatory authorities pursued policies geared towards ensuring the soundness of financial institutions, rather than policies designed to promote the innovation of financial technology. In contrast, it seems that the U.S. policy has been to encourage the innovation of financial technology to allow the development of various financial schemes and instruments, and to impose regulations only if and when problems arise. This policy stance, which had supposedly contributed to the development of securitization, caused grave problems.

Innovation and regulation must be well balanced. If the Japanese Government imposes overly stringent regulations, it will hamper financial innovation and cause the Japanese financial industry to decline. However, whenever any problematic microlevel financial phenomenon is observed, it is necessary to impose pre-emptive regulation before it develops into macrolevel behaviour. It is hoped that the financial administration will promote unrestricted innovation and develop the capacity to detect promptly problematic microlevel phenomena resulting from such innovation.

Difference Between the Chinese Stock Market Plunge and that of Post-bubble Japan

Chinese stock prices have fallen to one third of their peak level (see Figure 8.2), which was the case for Japanese stock prices in this country's post-bubble period. These two seemingly similar phenomena differ with respect to their impact on the banking sector, which has been far more limited in China than it was in Japan.

Partly due to their state-owned status, Chinese banks — unlike their counterparts in Japan — have rarely had large shareholdings, and therefore the impact on them from falling stock prices has been relatively small. In addition, at least for now, China has also not seen any huge plunge in land prices, which are reportedly supported by the government. In the United States, where banks had securitized mortgage loans to low-income borrowers and sold them as MBS to investors, many of these subprime debtors defaulted when housing prices fell. Thus, a number of MBS have gone sour, forcing investors, including banks, across the world to incur huge losses.

Government Measures to Avoid Triggering Credit Concerns in the Wake of the Financial Crisis

In Japan, a total of 180 financial institutions have failed since the end of the bubble, more specifically, in the period from 1991 through to 2008. They were mostly locally based

FIGURE 8.2
Movement of Share Prices on the Shanghai Stock Exchange

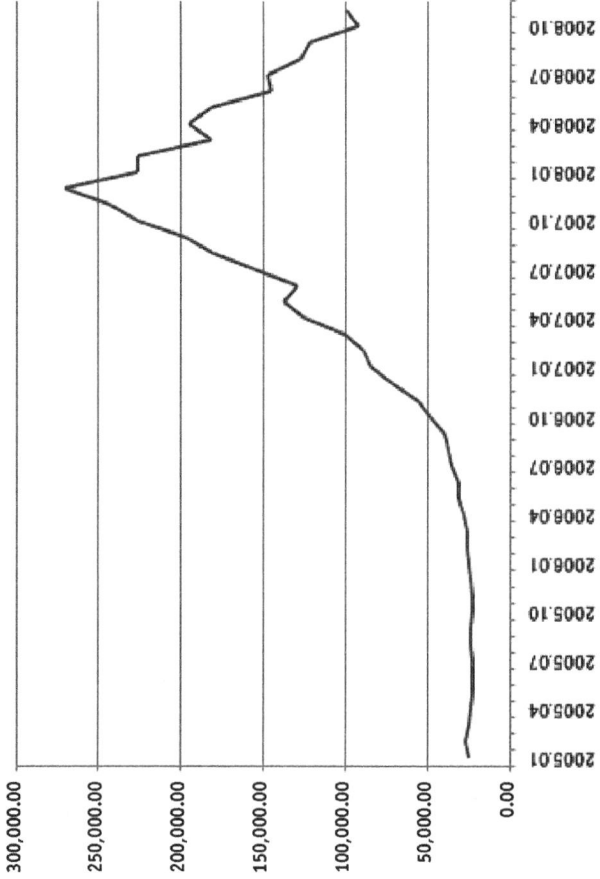

small institutions such as credit cooperatives, but some major banks were also included. This turmoil in the banking sector resulted in a credit crunch, which in turn delayed the recovery of the Japanese economy.

Despite initial opposition from Congress, the U.S. Government has so far: (i) raised the maximum amount of deposits covered by the Federal Deposit Insurance Corp. (FDIC) and introduced a temporary unlimited guarantee, such as the one introduced in Japan, on funds in non-interest-bearing transaction deposit accounts; and (ii) implemented a scheme to purchase bad assets from banks and inject public funds to recapitalize banks, prevent bank failures, and avoid systemic risk. In implementing and/or supporting these measures, the FDIC, the Department of Treasury, and the Federal Reserve Board generally acted in unison with one another, although some inconsistencies were observed in implementation methods.

So far the United States has responded to its crisis with much greater agility than did Japan to its banking crisis in the late 1990s. In Japan, in addition to measures comparable to (i) and (ii) above, the Financial Supervisory Agency (now the Financial Services Agency) monitored recapitalized banks' lending to ensure they were not squeezing off credit; and a special credit guarantee programme for small- and medium-sized enterprises (SMEs) — a scheme under which credit guarantee organizations provided 100 per cent coverage against losses sustained by banks from the bankruptcies of SME borrowers — was introduced to encourage banks to lend to SMEs.

However, this promise to cover 100 per cent of losses tempted some banks to take advantage of the scheme and lend to borrowers with unacceptably high risk profiles, resulting in a further increase in bad loans. In response to this new development, the percentage of loan losses covered by the scheme was lowered to 85 per cent so banks would be forced to bear part of the burden of a borrower's bankruptcy.

In Europe and the United Kingdom, governments have quickly enhanced their levels of deposit protection to avoid triggering credit concerns. They have also implemented measures to prevent banks from ceasing to function under the weight of bad loans and reduced capital levels, thus avoiding the route Japan followed towards prolonged economic stagnation.

Short-term Remedies and Medium- to Long-term Solutions

In the previous section I have discussed measures that were designed to avoid triggering credit concerns following the outbreak of a crisis, prevent large-scale withdrawals by panicky depositors, protect against credit squeezes by banks, and facilitate capital flows to corporations. These measures alone, however, cannot bring about an economic recovery. At the time of the Great Depression in the 1930s, many countries adopted Keynesian policies. In order to overcome the current crisis, developed countries are being urged to act in concert and embark on an aggressive fiscal policy, just like they did back in the 1930s.

However, with its public debt already at the level of 180 per cent of its gross domestic product (GDP), Japan finds itself increasingly restricted from issuing government bonds to finance fiscal stimulus measures. Thus, Japan needs to utilize private sector funds to finance its fiscal measures. And the same applies to countries such as China and India, where infrastructure remains underdeveloped.

Keynesian policies typically call for the financing of fiscal stimulus with the issuance of government bonds during bad times. However, for countries with enormous fiscal deficits, such as Japan, it is extremely difficult to issue additional government bonds because there are few economic entities with the capacity to purchase them. In Japan, government bonds are mostly held by financial institutions.

Issuing revenue bonds is one way to utilize private sector funds. This scheme is applicable to the construction of revenue-generating infrastructure. Revenue bonds can be issued to raise private sector funds to help finance a specific infrastructure project, such as the construction of a highway. Both the principal and interest portions of these bonds are then repaid solely from revenue generated by the same infrastructure project, such as tolls in the case of a highway. The government typically bears a portion of the construction costs, with the remaining costs financed by private sector funds raised through the issuance of revenue bonds.

The extent to which a specific infrastructure project is financed by private sector funds is based on the expected revenue from the project to be constructed, with the expected return on investment equal to or greater than the rate of return on government bonds. In cases where actual revenue exceeds the initial expectation, investors would receive a higher return. At the same time, the scheme needs to be designed in such a way that the operator of the infrastructure project, for example, a highway corporation, would also benefit from the higher-than-expected revenue so it would have an incentive to boost earnings. It is also possible to set a government guaranteed minimum rate of return for revenue bonds.

In some Asian countries, notably China and India, domestic demand will increase when their economies are revitalized through efficient infrastructure development. These countries have the potential to serve as long-term global growth engines, capable of generating demand for goods and services produced across the world. Not only developed countries, but also developing countries should be implementing aggressive fiscal policies to help prevent the world from slipping into depression. In doing so, they can exclude wasteful public works projects by making use of private sector funds, which by design should flow only into highly profitable projects.

Keynesian policies come under fierce criticism during periods of economic growth, yet are much more popular in times such as during the global financial crisis when the private sector economy is in a sharp downswing. In dealing with the ongoing situation, governments will, it is hoped, steer clear of outdated Keynesian policies and instead pursue new Keynesian policies that take advantage of private sector funds.

Certain public projects, water and sewerage services, compulsory education, etc., must obviously be implemented regardless of their profitability in order to ensure national minimum standards. But these projects can also take advantage of revenue bonds when some sort of fee income is expected, as is the case for water and sewerage services. Such projects can be partially funded from tax revenues, with the remaining amount supplied by private sector funds (see Figure 8.3). The use of private sector funds, albeit

FIGURE 8.3
Leveraging Private Sector Funds for
Infrastructure Development

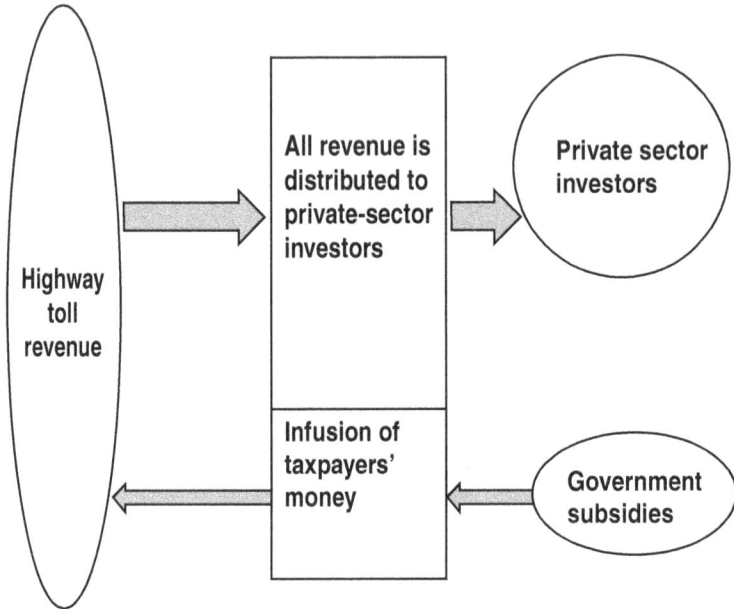

partially, would improve the profitability of the project due to their profit seeking nature. At the same time, the project's profit performance would become visible to the market and the management of water and sewerage services would become subject to external monitoring.

In the example shown in Figure 8.3, government tax revenues cover 30 per cent of the cost of operating a highway, and the remaining 70 per cent is provided by private sector funds. In this scenario, all the toll revenue generated from the highway operations is distributed to the private sector investors at a rate of return on investment equal to 10/7, with the rate being augmented by the infusion of tax revenue.

There is great hope that emerging economies, such as China and India, will launch new Keynesian initiatives leveraging private sector funds and become the new engines of global growth that will drive the world economy to growth and prosperity once again.

Index

www.ingramcontent.com/pod-product-compliance
Lightning Source LLC
Chambersburg PA
CBHW020751300326
41914CB00050B/119